CW01666119

MATTHIAS STOM

Isaac blessing Jacob

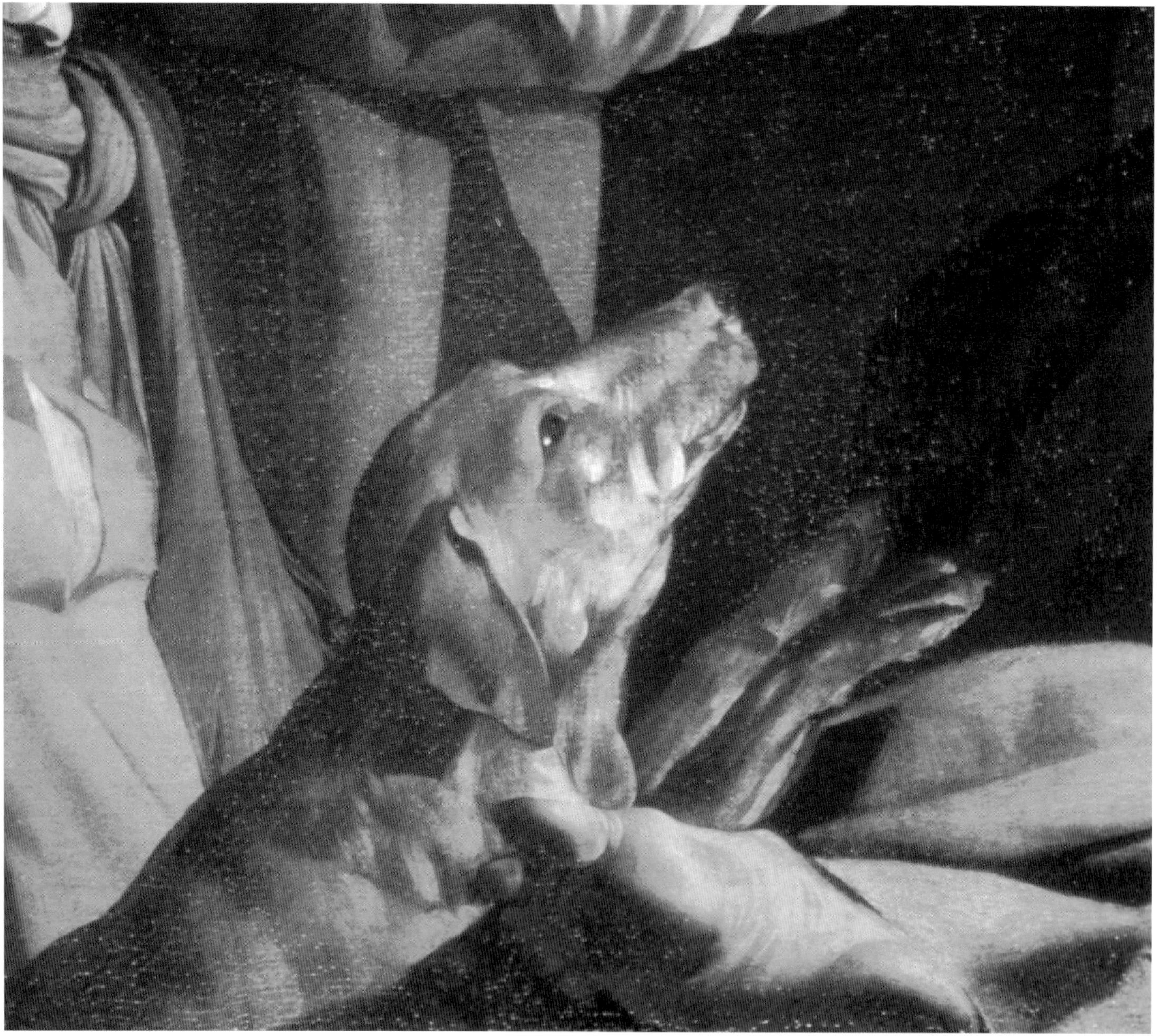

MATTHIAS STOM

Isaac blessing Jacob

Richard Verdi

The Barber Institute of Fine Arts
The University of Birmingham
29 October 1999 – 16 January 2000

Front cover:
Matthias Stom, *Isaac blessing Jacob* (detail) The Barber Institute of Fine Arts, The University of Birmingham
Matthias Stom, *Christ disputing with the Doctors* (detail) Collection of Mr. A. Alfred Taubman

Frontispiece:
Matthias Stom, *Isaac blessing Jacob* (detail)

ISBN 0 9537051 0 2
Richard Verdi

Project management by Magnolia Concept, Warwickshire
Designed by Krome, Cambridgeshire
Set by Set Two, Cambridgeshire
Printed in England by Edward Fox & Son Limited

Contents

Preface

The paintings of Matthias Stom are instantly recognisable; the artist himself, almost totally unknown. What seasoned museum-goer has failed to be impressed by Stom's demonstrative style – the over-excited figures, wearing expressions of amazement, their eyes bulging, brows furrowed and fingers flared? Painted in fiery reds and golds, set alight by the glow of a ubiquitous candle, Stom's saints, shepherds and patriarchs are among the most readily identifiable images of seventeenth-century art, reappearing from picture to picture with a consistency and quality that makes the attribution of his works remarkably easy. Admittedly, this repetitiveness can be wearisome and once led the greatest scholar on the artist, Benedict Nicolson, to declare that 'a full-scale Stom(er) exhibition would be a catastrophe'. Seen in great numbers, there is little doubt that the artist's paintings might strike the average art lover as variations on a single theme. Yet hidden beneath Stom's evident limitations is a distinctive and highly original style which makes him one of the most audaciously dramatic artists of his time. But he also remains among the most elusive; and the reasons for this are easily told.

An itinerant Dutchman, who is first recorded in Rome and then worked in the artistic 'backwaters' of Naples and Sicily, Stom is among the greatest art historical mysteries. Basing his style on that of Caravaggio, at a time when the latter's influence was in decline, he attracted few public commissions and – unlike nearly all other Dutchmen who worked in Italy – he never returned to make his mark in his native land. As a result, Stom led a stateless and undocumented existence, and may also have endured one other handicap which concealed him from history's glare. In Dutch, 'Stom' means deaf mute. Is it possible that the artist suffered from this further impediment to having his deeds and movements recorded? We will never know. All that is certain is that he is first mentioned as Stomer, whereas his rare signatures tell us that it was the shortened form of this name he preferred. Lost from view from his death in c. 1652 to the early years of the twentieth century, his career has been reconstructed by art historians, aided by his eminently identifiable paintings. But the uncertainties that surround all aspects of his life and work are evident in the catalogue that follows, which abounds in words like 'may', 'could have', 'impossible' and 'unclear'. To have done otherwise would have been to lay claim to what we do not – and probably never will – possess.

This is the first exhibition ever devoted to Matthias Stom and centres around one of his undisputed masterpieces, *Isaac blessing Jacob*, which was acquired by the Barber Institute of Fine Arts in 1994 with generous assistance from the National Art Collections Fund and the Museums and Galleries Commission/Victoria and Albert Museum Purchase Grant Fund. The exhibition is the fourth in a series devoted to major works in the Institute's collection. It was preceded by *Nicolas Poussin, 'Tancred and Erminia'* (Birmingham Museum and Art Gallery, 1992), *Thomas Gainsborough, 'The Harvest Wagon'* (Birmingham Museum and Art Gallery and Art Gallery of Ontario, Toronto, 1995) and *Simone Martini, 'St John the Evangelist'* (Barber Institute of Fine Arts, 1998). But, whereas Poussin, Gainsborough, and even Simone Martini require no introduction to the art-loving public, Matthias Stom emphatically does. For this reason, the exhibition includes nearly all of the paintings by him in public and private collections in the United Kingdom and also considers his early importance for developments in British art, through the inclusion of *Salome receiving the Head of John the Baptist* and the copy of this by William Dobson, which are shown together for the first time since the latter was painted in c. 1640. But the focus of the exhibition is *Isaac blessing Jacob*, which is reunited with its pendant, *Christ disputing with the Doctors*. The former is an unusual subject for Stom and lacks the exaggerated theatricality which he so often favoured. Instead, as a tale of secrecy and subterfuge, it elicited from the artist one of his most psychologically intense and profound works. This is shown with a range of other treatments of the theme by his predecessors and contemporaries, which place the Barber Institute's picture in a wider context. The result is no substitute for a larger Stom exhibition – which, if judiciously selected, need not be a 'catastrophe' – and omits whole areas of his work. Among them are his pre-Caravaggesque pictures, which are irrelevant to *Isaac blessing Jacob*, and the paintings of his Sicilian phase, the majority of which are too large for the Institute's walls. It is hoped nevertheless that the exhibition will serve to introduce Stom to a wider audience as an artist of compelling power and originality who is fully deserving of our admiration and delight after nearly four centuries of neglect.

Acknowledgements

Although this is a very modestly sized exhibition, it is also the largest ever to be mounted at the Barber Institute of Fine Arts, which was prevented from holding any exhibitions by the terms of the original Trust Deed – a restriction that was only altered in 1997. In practical terms, this means that certain members of the Institute's staff have suddenly found themselves co-opted onto its exhibitions team, while still being required to fulfil their normal duties. I am especially grateful to Paul Spencer-Longhurst, Senior Curator of the Institute, for his invaluable advice and assistance on all aspects of the exhibition, and to Rosemary Poynton, Acting Registrar, for her tireless efforts in assisting with its realisation on a practical level. As ever, I am indebted to the Trustees of the Institute for their continuing support and encouragement towards the exhibitions programme. Thanks are also due to Yvonne Locke, who typed the entire catalogue with exemplary speed and efficiency, and to John Brooks, John McDill, Sophie Wilson, and Sarah Jennings for their energetic support of the project. I am grateful, too, to Sue Fryer and Peter Owen for their respective roles in designing and producing the catalogue and in devising a visual identity for the exhibition.

Further from home, I am greatly indebted to Henry Avar, Alfred and Ronald Cohen, Brian Sewell, Leonard Slatkes and Luisa Vertova for generously sharing their knowledge and enthusiasm of Stom with me during the preparatory stages of the exhibition. Iva Lisikewycz and Ulrich Graf Arco-Zinneberg were instrumental in securing two of the key loans for the exhibition. But my chief debt inevitably is to those institutions and individuals who have loaned to the exhibition, many of whom also incurred an unforeseen obligation through their extraordinary generosity. Since this is a pioneering venture, the majority of paintings included in it have never been requested for loan. As a result, a high proportion of them have been specially cleaned for the occasion, making it possible for Stom's first monographic exhibition to show him at his very best.

Richard Verdi
Director,
The Barber Institute of Fine Arts

List of Lenders

The Duke of Devonshire and the Chatsworth Settlement Trustees 18
Count Harrach Family Collection, Schloss Rohrau, Lower Austria 11
Sir Denis Mahon 5
Brian Sewell 4
Mr. A. Alfred Taubman 2
Trafalgar Galleries, London 9
Private Collection, United Kingdom 7
Rijksmuseum, Amsterdam 10
The Barber Institute of Fine Arts, The University of Birmingham 1, 21, 23
Birmingham Museums and Art Gallery 8
Kingston Lacy, The Bankes Collection (The National Trust) 3
Leeds Museums and Galleries (Temple Newsam House) 6
Board of Trustees of the National Museums and Galleries on Merseyside (Walker Art Gallery, Liverpool) 12, 19, 22
The British Museum, London 13, 14, 16, 17
Courtauld Gallery, London (Witt Collection) 20
Ashmolean Museum, Oxford 15

Abbreviations

The following abbreviations are used throughout the catalogue:

Nicolson 1977 Benedict Nicolson, 'Stomer brought up-to-date', *The Burlington Magazine*, CXIX, April 1977, pp. 230–45.

Nicolson 1989 Benedict Nicolson, *Caravaggism in Europe*, second edition, Turin, 1989. 3 vols. (Nos. refer to the list of works by Stom, Vol. I, pp. 179–88.)

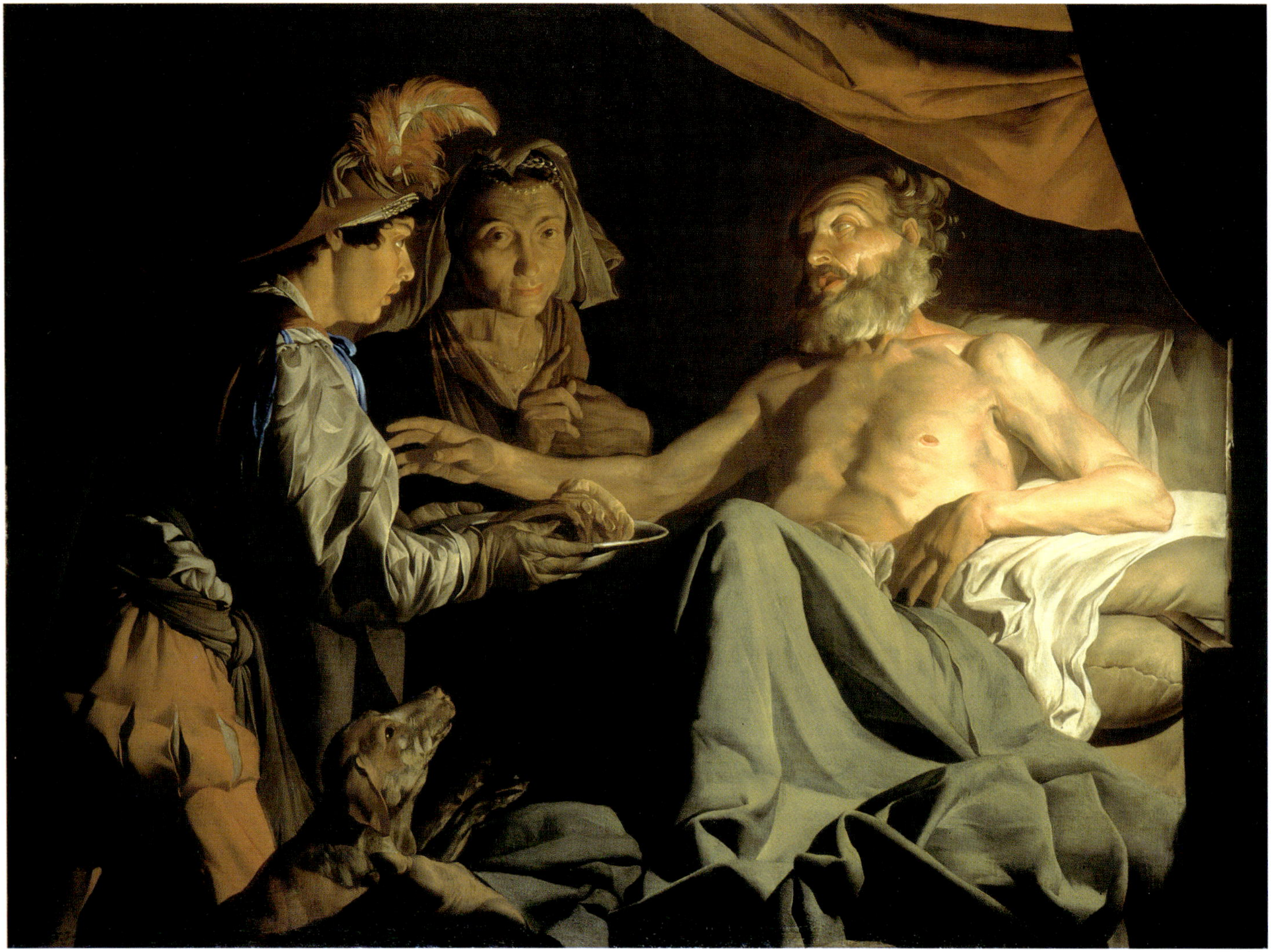

Fig.1 (No.1), Matthias Stom, *Isaac blessing Jacob*,
The Barber Institute of Fine Arts, The University of Birmingham

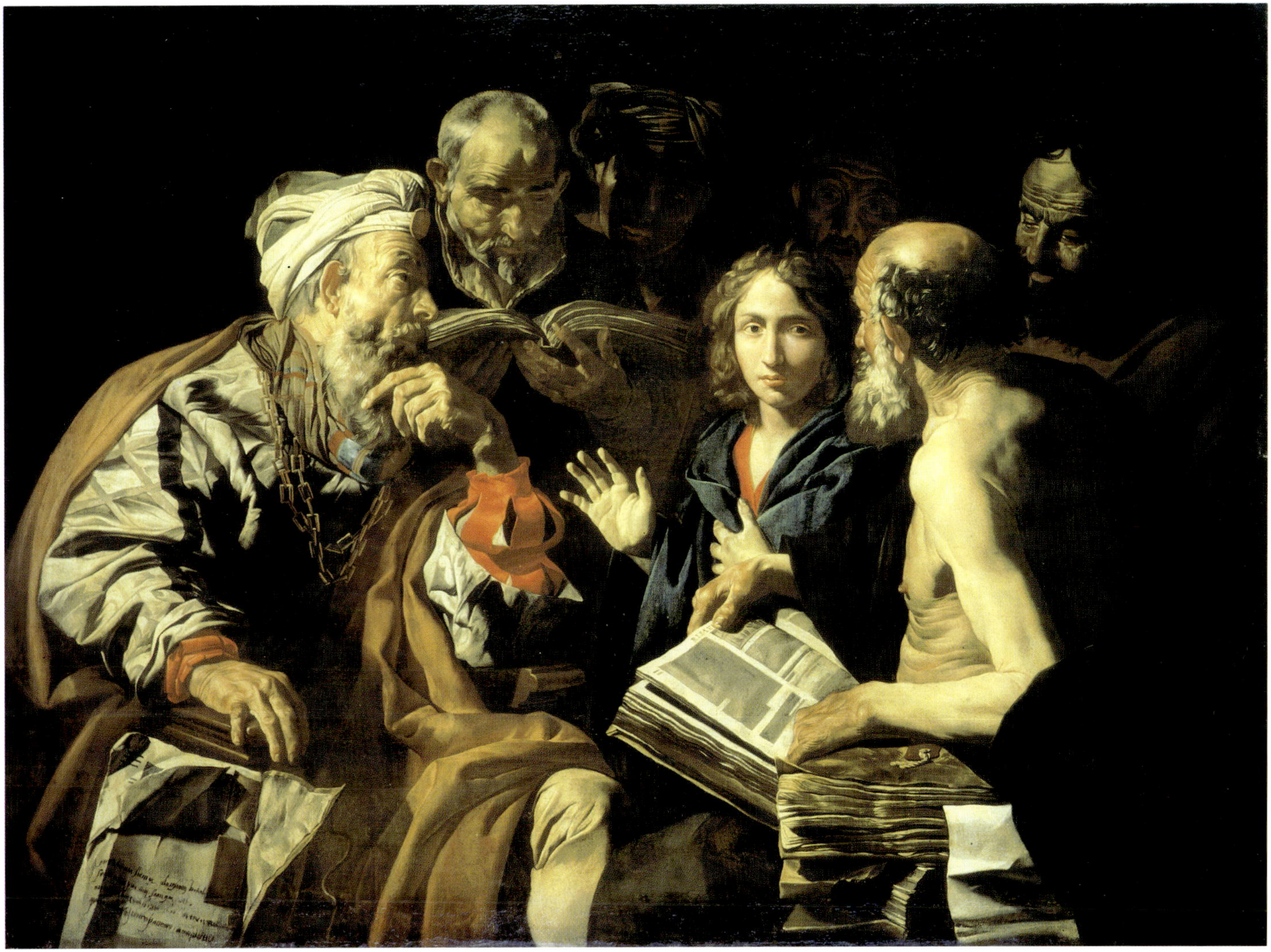

Fig.2 (No.2), Matthias Stom, *Christ disputing with the Doctors*,
Collection of Mr. A. Alfred Taubman

MATTHIAS STOM (c. 1600 –? after 1652)

His life

Matthias Stom is first documented in Rome in 1630, living in the Strada dell' Ormo, in the parish of S Nicola in Arcione.[1] His age is given as 30, indicating that he was born around the turn of the century, c.1600. He was still living at the same address in 1631 and 1632, but then disappears from view. In 1692, a number of night scenes by him are recorded in the Capuchin Church of S Efremo Nuovo, Naples.[2] Since many other paintings by him also bear a Neapolitan provenance – including *Isaac blessing Jacob* (fig.1) – this fact, together with the style of his works, has led all scholars to deduce that he spent a number of years in Naples, perhaps from c.1633 to c. 1640. He is next documented in Sicily in 1641, where he executed his only signed and dated work, an altarpiece of the *Miracle of St Isidore Agricola* for the high altar of the church of the Agostiniani in Caccamo, near Palermo. Between 1646 and 1649 he painted three canvases for the important Sicilian collector, Antonio Ruffo, Duke of Messina, who also owned works by Titian, van Dyck and Ribera and was to commission three paintings from Rembrandt in the 1650s and '60s.[3] On stylistic evidence, he is regarded as the painter of a large altarpiece of the *Assumption of the Virgin* executed for the church of Santa Maria Assunta, Chiuduno, near Bergamo, in 1652.[4] This suggests that he may have left Sicily and ended his career in northern Italy. It may be significant that one member of a late-seventeenth century family of painters of battle scenes and landscapes active in Venice and northern Italy was named Mathäus (or Matteo) Stom. Born in 1643, he died in Verona in 1702, and may have been the artist's son.[5]

In addition to the Caccamo altarpiece, Stom signed two other canvases, a *Tobias and the Angel* (Bredius Museum, The Hague; fig. 3) and a *Martyrdom of St Cecilia*, formerly in the church of the Cappuccini, Messina, which was destroyed in the earthquake of 1908. All of these works are inscribed with the form 'Stom', indicating that the more familiar name 'Stomer' was not favoured by the artist. It occurs for the first time in a printed source of 1692.[6]

Nothing is known of the place of Stom's birth, though he is traditionally claimed to have come from Amersfoort, 20km north east of Utrecht. This is founded on the fact that, in 1625, the Amersfoort-born painter Paulus Bor inhabited the same house in Rome that Stom occupied in 1630, which suggests that the two men may have known one another. In the literature on the artist, Stom is often described as a pupil of the leading Caravaggesque painter in Utrecht, Gerrit van Honthorst (1590-1656).[7] Since the latter only returned to Utrecht from Rome in 1620, this is unlikely to be strictly true. Stom almost certainly began his apprenticeship earlier than this, probably around 1614–15. As we shall see, however, his style reveals connections with the art of both Utrecht and Antwerp and suggests that, even before he reached Italy, he may have led an itinerant life.

His work

Nearly 200 paintings survive which may be attributed to Stom.[8] About three-quarters of these treat biblical themes, the majority from the New Testament and the lives of the saints. The remainder depict subjects from mythology, ancient history and everyday life. The last category consists almost entirely of half-length depictions of one or two figures lit by an artificial light source such as a candle or firebrand, like the *Old Woman and Boy by Candlelight* exhibited here (fig. 22). On stylistic grounds, it would appear that Stom produced works in all of these categories throughout his career; and it is noteworthy that the three paintings by the artist acquired by Ruffo in the late 1640s were a *Death of Cato*, a *Denial of St Peter* and a

Head of a Man and Woman, which encompass all the major themes of his art.[9]

Since only one of Stom's works is dated, his creative development is impossible to determine from documentary evidence alone. In place of this, two other criteria have been applied in devising a working chronology of the artist's career: namely, the style and provenance of his pictures. Neither of these is an infallible guide, and the latter may be particularly unreliable given that pictures moved freely between centres as close as Naples, Sicily and Malta – where four major works by Stom are still to be seen – in the seventeenth century. Fortunately, however, Stom's surviving works fall into several distinct stylistic categories, first defined by Benedict Nicolson in a key article of 1977,[10] which forms the basis for the following discussion. Until further documentary evidence emerges, this is likely to remain the standard account of the artist's development. As Nicolson himself observed:[11]

> *Stomer no longer presents us with problems of attribution. He will never mislead us by rising to the heights; will never take wing on a gust of air, strong enough to transform his vision of life and hence his style so that it becomes unrecognisable, as an artist of genius will do. He cultivates a well-trimmed garden …*

Given this degree of predictability throughout his career, internal stylistic evidence makes it possible to chart a progression which appears remarkably logical.

One phenomenon is apparent throughout much of Stom's oeuvre: namely that, as Nicolson concluded, 'he repeats himself over and over again.' In addition to producing many variants on the same theme throughout his career, he was also inclined to combine elements from different pictures when fashioning new works and even to adapt strikingly similar compositions to suit totally different themes. An example of this last practice is the close relationship between *Isaac blessing Jacob* (fig. 1) and *Sarah bringing Hagar to Abraham* (fig. 15). While such expedients may be explained by his relatively limited inventive powers, they may also have been forced upon the artist by the need to work at great speed. For it is noteworthy that, during the two decades of his Italian career, Stom was extraordinarily prolific, executing over 150 paintings, many of which were on a very large scale – a rate of production that would have necessitated a certain creative economy in any but the most prodigiously gifted master.

Two other characteristics are common to virtually all of Stom's paintings and may be seen as unchanging features of his artistic personality. The first is a decided fondness for posing his figures close to the picture plane and providing them with little (if any) setting, a device which intensifies the boldness and immediacy of his art. The second is a distinct tendency to align his forms and figures parallel to the confines of the frame, in rigidly constrained poses. This often has the effect of increasing the tension of his compositions and further enhances their dramatic impact.

These features aside, Stom's surviving works may be divided into two distinct groups of vastly unequal size. By far the larger is that group which reveals clearly the influence of Caravaggio in its dramatic play of light and shade, warm saturated colours and plebeian figure types. A much smaller group consists of works of an altogether different tonality, showing figures in broad, silvery daylight and employing a range of paler hues – lemon yellows, soft pinks and light blues.[12] To understand how these two groups may relate to one another, it is necessary to attempt a hypothetical reconstruction of the artist's early career.

Assuming that Stom's creative training followed that of other Netherlandish painters of his day, he must have been apprenticed to his first master in his mid-teens, around 1614-15 – the age when Rubens and Rembrandt also entered this position, and several years after the clearly precocious van Dyck, who is recorded as working with his

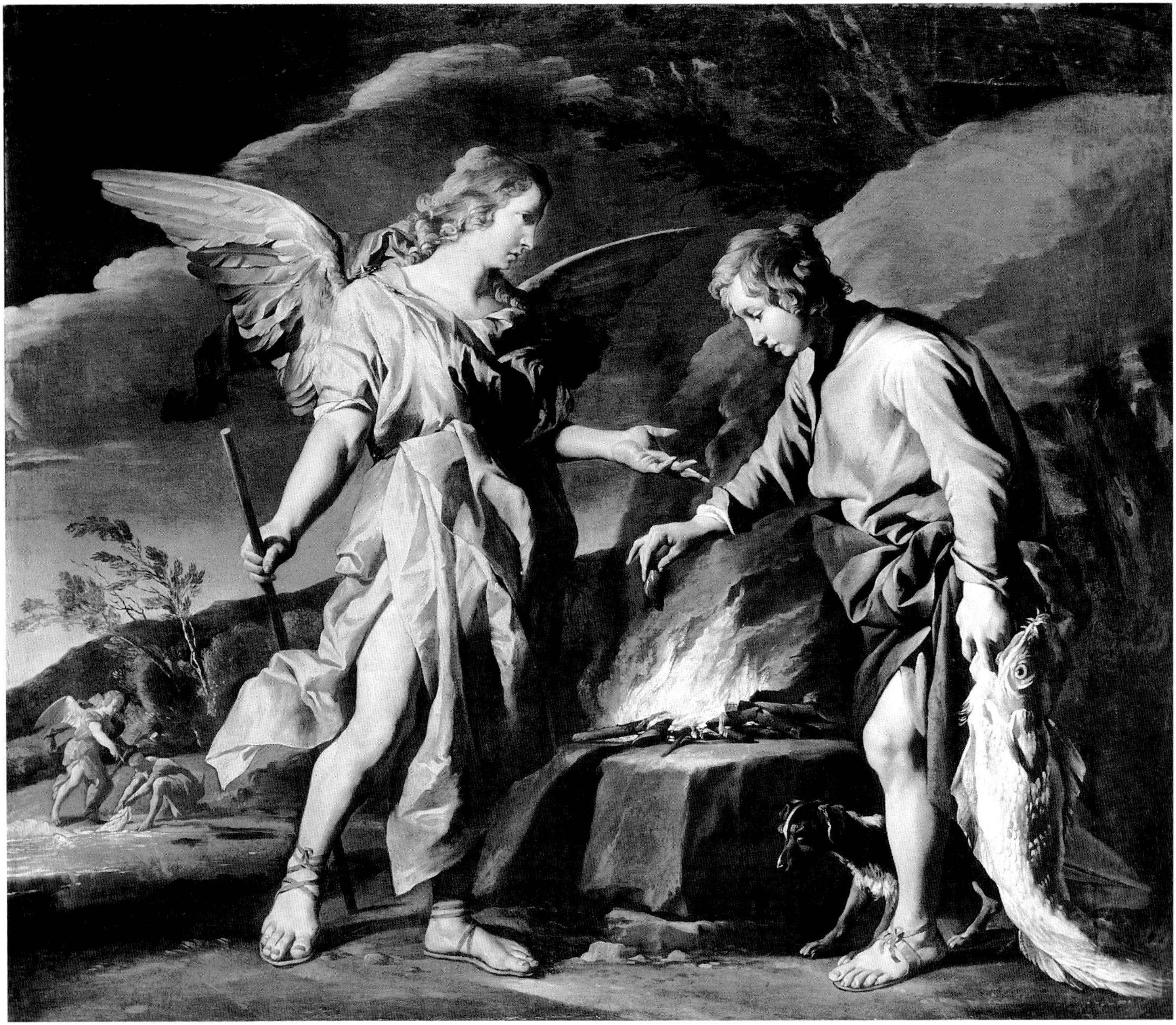

Fig. 3, Matthias Stom, *Tobias and the Angel*,
Bredius Museum, The Hague

master, Hendrick van Balen, at the age of only ten. Though it is impossible to know who Stom's first teacher was – or where he practised – it is certain that he would have worked in a pre-Caravaggesque style, since Caravaggism only reached the Netherlands with the return to Utrecht of Hendrick Terbrugghen (1588–1629) in 1616, Gerrit van Honthorst (1590–1656) in 1620 and Dirck van Baburen (c.1595–1624), probably in the following year. Before their arrival, the dominant style in the United Provinces was that of the mannerist painters, Abraham Bloemaert (1566–1651) and Joachim Wtewael (1566–1638), who worked in Utrecht, where the former taught both Terbrugghen and Honthorst before their journeys to Italy. Characteristic of the styles of both Bloemaert and Wtewael of these years is a decided fondness for light, bright and somewhat metallic colours and for silvery daylight scenes, as may also be found in such non-Caravaggesque works by Stom as *Tobias and the Angel* (fig. 3). On circumstantial grounds, therefore, it is likely – but by no means certain – that this small group of pictures by the artist predates the nocturnal scenes for which he has become much better known. They may even have originated as early as the late 1610s or early 1620s; and it is noteworthy that one of them – an *Adoration of the Magi* in Stockholm – contains clear reminiscences of two works on the same theme by Terbrugghen (Rijksmuseum, Amsterdam) and Bloemaert (Centraal Museum, Utrecht), which are respectively dated 1619 and 1624.

In addition to their prevailing colour and tonality, the group of pictures just discussed also bears another distinctive stylistic trait. This is the purity and fullness of their forms, together with their smooth and idealised facial types. Draperies tend to be broad and voluminous and the figures neatly coiffured in tight, wavy locks, which Nicolson likened to tin foil. The exuberance of this style bears some resemblances to Flemish art of the 1610s and leads one to wonder if Stom journeyed to Antwerp during these years, where the robust and extrovert art of Rubens, Abraham Janssens and the early Jordaens prevailed; and there are clear circumstantial connections with all of these masters in a number of his works.[13] What is also undeniable is that certain of these Flemish features persist in some of Stom's Caravaggesque canvases, among them the *Satyr with Peasant Family* (fig. 18) and *Salome receiving the Head of John the Baptist* (fig. 12). Assuming that the artist's career *did* follow a logical trajectory, these pictures have some claims to be regarded as his earliest nocturnes, executed in the Netherlands under the sudden impact of the return of the three great Dutch Caravaggesque painters to Utrecht, which effected a dramatic stylistic change upon much of Dutch art, including that of Frans Hals and the young Rembrandt.

When Nicolson devised his hypothetical reconstruction of Stom's career, he allocated only two works to the artist's pre-Roman years, one of which was the *Man with a Glass of Wine, Pipe and Fiddle* exhibited here (fig. 4). These he sensibly concluded had been painted in Utrecht – the centre of Dutch Caravaggesque painting – in c.1625-9, immediately before the artist's journey to Italy. While so cautionary an approach is understandable when dealing with an artist as elusive as Stom, it is hard to imagine that he did not paint much more than this if we assume that he completed his training in the late 1610s. In addition to the group of 'blonde' canvases modelled on Bloemaert and Wtewael, which numbers more than a dozen works, he is also likely to have executed some Caravaggesque pictures prior to his visit to Rome. When one considers that Bloemaert himself was 'converted' to Caravaggism almost immediately after the return of his erstwhile pupils from Italy,[14] it is likely that the younger and (presumably) more impressionable Stom followed a similar path. But precisely what he painted in the years between 1620 and 1629 remains impossible to determine; for even those pictures by him which are manifestly indebted to works by Honthorst, Terbrugghen or Baburen – and there are many! – *could* have been executed 'belatedly' from memories of their canvases once he had reached Italy.

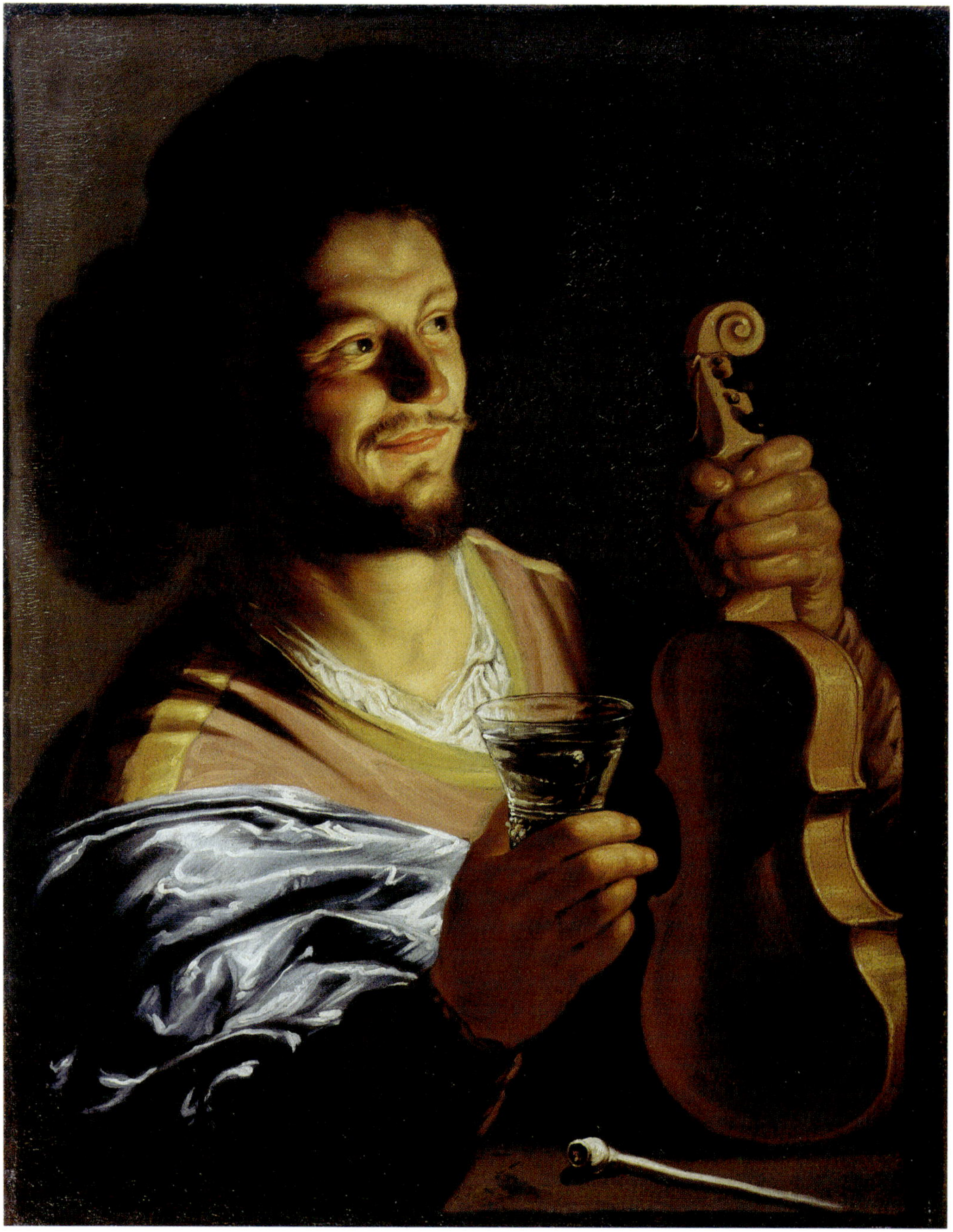

Fig. 4 (No. 3), Matthias Stom,
A Man with a Glass of Wine, Pipe and Fiddle,
Kingston Lacy, The Bankes Collection (The National Trust)

There are three features of Stom's art which suggest, however, that he was already painting Caravaggesque works before his departure for Italy. The first of these is the relatively large number of genre scenes he executed throughout his career. Though such themes occur in the art of Caravaggio and his Italian followers, they are much more frequently encountered among the Utrecht Caravaggisti, who directly inspired a number of similar works by Stom. This provides circumstantial evidence that his interest in such subjects was already kindled from his earliest years. The other two features link his art specifically with that of Honthorst – the one master to whom Stom's works were most often attributed before his own artistic personality was identified and defined. These are his penchant for candlelight scenes and the prevailing colour harmonies of his works. The former are commonly found among Honthorst's Caravaggesque works and noticeably rarer in the art of Caravaggio's Italian followers.[15] Since a number of Stom's candlelight scenes are variants on those by Honthorst, this suggests a close engagement with the art of the latter from an early moment in Stom's career. The colour harmonies favoured by both artists are likewise very similar and reveal a distinct preference for the warm end of the spectrum, with reds, yellows, golds and browns – the colours of flame itself – prevailing over all other hues. To be sure, Stom's palette is readily distinguishable from that of Honthorst and is, if anything, even more fiery, in its coppery flesh tones, warm brick reds, and shimmering greys and blues. But the earthy and autumnal colour harmonies encountered in both masters link them more closely with one another than with any of their Caravaggesque contemporaries. Taken together, these connections strongly suggest that certain of the key characteristics of Stom's style had already been established before he crossed the Alps, under the direct influence of the most celebrated of the Utrecht Caravaggisti, Honthorst.

We are on firmer ground when we move to Rome, where Stom first encountered the art of Caravaggio and of those of his followers whose works could still be seen in the Eternal City. Among these were a number of important early canvases that Honthorst and Baburen had executed for Roman patrons, several of which were to have a decisive impact upon Stom's own art. The most notable of these were Honthorst's *Christ before the High Priest* (fig. 21) and *Liberation of St Peter* (Gemäldegalerie, Berlin), both of which were commissioned by the Marchese Giustiniani in the late 1610s. The former provided the source for Stom's two paintings of *Christ before Pilate* (fig. 20) and *Christ before the High Priest* (Private Collection) and the latter for his own *Liberation of St Peter* (Kunsthaus, Zurich), which is among the most unashamedly derivative of all his works. This suggests that it may be a product of his early Roman years.

What prompted Stom to leave Rome after only two years is impossible to say; but what can be stated with some confidence is that, had he not done so, he would soon have been out of work. For, by the early 1630s, Caravaggesque painting had all but died out in Rome, to be replaced by a more exuberantly baroque style, epitomised by the art of Pietro da Cortona. Nor could Stom have maintained this style had he returned to Utrecht; for, there too, it was a spent force, with both Baburen and Terbrugghen dead and Honthorst himself working in a dramatically altered and more classicizing style and increasingly based outside Utrecht, in England (1628) and The Hague (from 1630). Thus, the only places where Stom would have found favour for his art at this time were where he went – to Naples and (eventually) Sicily - where Caravaggio himself had preceded him and where there was still a group of artists, including the great Spanish master, Jusepe de Ribera (1591 – 1652), inspired by the trenchant realism and dramatic lighting pioneered by Caravaggio.

It is only with Stom's Neapolitan and Sicilian works that one is reasonably certain of an approximate date of origin, at least for a core group of pictures. The reasons for this hinge on their physical size and provenance. As Nicolson noted, all of Stom's major biblical and classical canvases with Sicilian provenances are executed on a vast scale when compared with their counterparts traceable to Neapolitan collections. From this he astutely observed 'that Stomer was patronised on a more lavish scale in Sicily than ever before.'[16] Though it would be unwise to deduce from this that he painted no smaller works during these years, this hypothesis seems entirely convincing and is supported by the fact that Stom's only two surviving altarpieces date from the later years of his career.

In addition to the greater dimensions that characterise Stom's Sicilian paintings there are several other stylistic features of these works that distinguish them from the works executed in Naples. The most obvious of these is the correspondingly greater ambitiousness of their compositions, which typically consist of a large number of highly-strung figures in violently dramatic poses, which at times threaten to rend the design apart. Coupled with this increased virtuosity is a greater exaggeration in the description of individual figures. Human flesh is rendered as lined and furrowed and bears a consistency that Nicolson appropriately likened to baked clay. Facial expression is pushed to extremes and occasionally borders on a grimace. And draperies themselves fall in tense, angular and agitated folds, further heightening the voltage. Though this style runs the risk of appearing bombastic, at its best, as in the *Capture of Christ* (fig. 5), it can possess an explosive dramatic power which seems almost cinematic and imbues Stom's works of this phase with a near-threatening intensity.

By a process of deduction, the pictures of the preceding, Neapolitan years appear more normative and restrained. A higher proportion of them are based on Caravaggesque prototypes and many depict themes directly associated with Caravaggio himself, such as the Adoration of the Shepherds or the Supper at Emmaus. Poses appear more moderate and gestures less flamboyant; flesh less wrinkled and petrified; and the draperies are arranged in broad, cascading folds which appear *moderato* rather than *agitato*. All of these features lend to these works a classic and unforced authority. In short, they are the quintessential Stoms – works in which the theatrical devices of the Caravaggesques are tempered by a love of intimacy and individuality inherited from the North. It goes without saying, however, that no precise line of demarcation can be drawn between the works of the artist's Roman, Neapolitan, and Sicilian years, and that what (if anything) he created in northern Italy during the last phase of his career remains shrouded in mystery. But it is reasonably certain that the picture which forms the focus of the present exhibition is a product of his years in Naples.

ISAAC BLESSING JACOB

The theme before Stom

In Genesis XXVII the Bible tells the story of the contest between Jacob and Esau to receive the paternal blessing from their aged father Isaac. Prior to their birth, Isaac had enquired of the Lord whether his wife, Rebecca, would bear him any children and was assured that she would bear twins, who would give their names to two nations, and that he who was born second should excel the elder. At their birth Esau, who was rough and hairy, emerged first, with Jacob – who was smooth – clinging to his heel. Though Isaac preferred his firstborn, Rebecca favoured Jacob – the Lord's own favourite – and the rivalry between the sons took a decisive turn when Esau sold his birthright to his brother in return for a mess of pottage, a subject that was repeatedly portrayed by artists, among them Terbrugghen, Stom and Rembrandt.

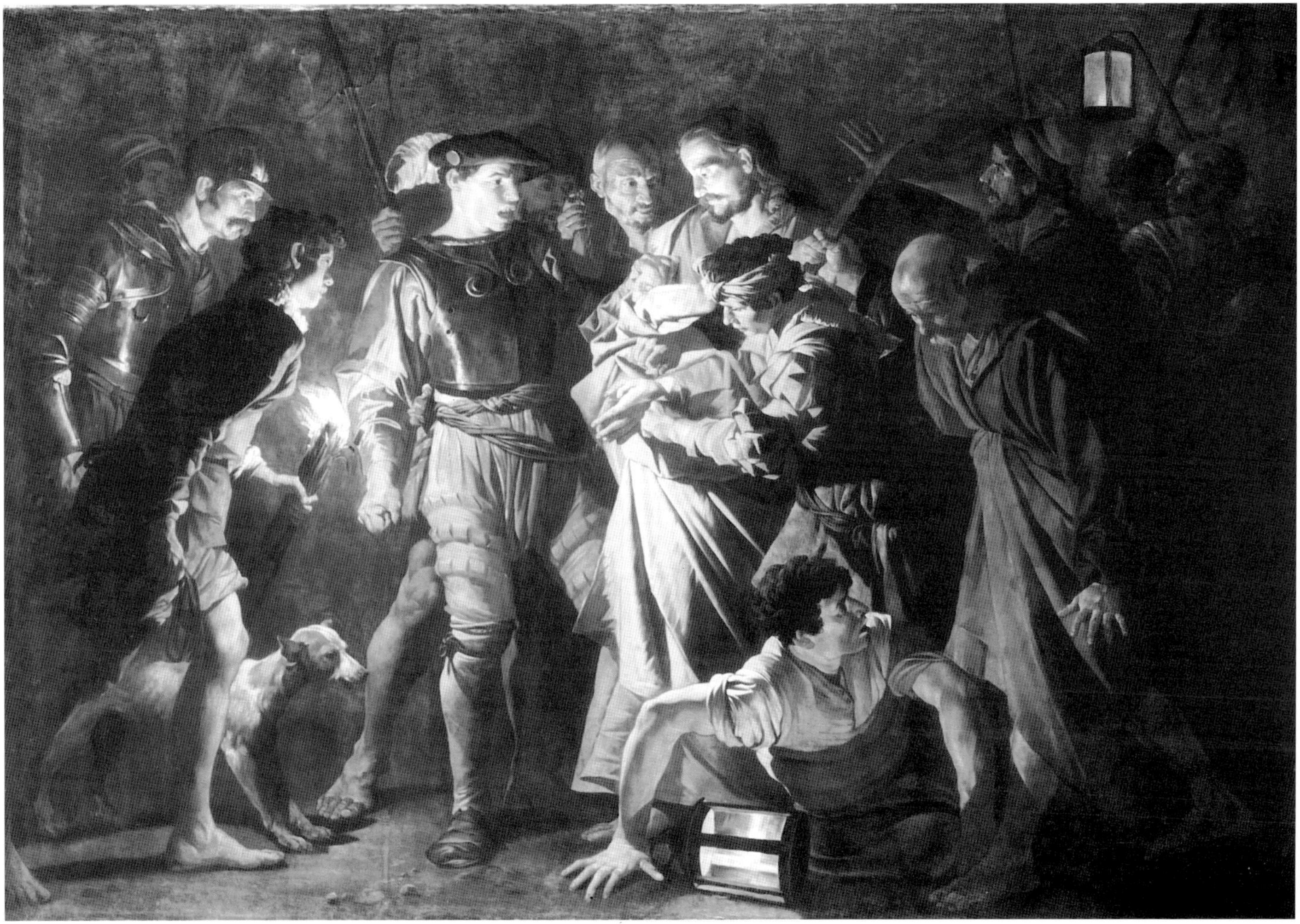

Fig. 5, Matthias Stom, *The Capture of Christ*,
The National Gallery of Ireland, Dublin

On his deathbed, Isaac – his eyes dimmed with age – summons Esau to bestow upon him the blessing that will give him priority over his brother. Bidding him to take up his weapons and hunt for some venison, he asks Esau to prepare from this a meal so that he may eat before blessing his son. When Rebecca overhears this conversation, she instructs Jacob to kill two kids from which she will make savoury meat for Isaac. Dressing Jacob up in Esau's fine clothes, she then completes the disguise by wrapping the skins of the goats around Jacob's hands, so that he will resemble his hairy brother.

The meal prepared, Jacob presents it to his father:

And Isaac said unto his son, How is it that thou hast found it so quickly, my son? And he said, Because the Lord thy God brought it to me.

And Isaac said unto Jacob, Come near, I pray thee, that I may feel thee, my son, whether thou be my very son Esau or not.

And Jacob went near unto Isaac his father; and he felt him, and said, The voice is Jacob's voice, but the hands are the hands of Esau.

And he discerned him not, because his hands were hairy, as his brother Esau's hands: so he blessed him.

And he said, Art thou my very son Esau? And he said, I am.

And he said, Bring it near to me, and I will eat of my son's venison, that my soul may bless thee. And he brought it near to him, and he did eat: and he brought him wine, and he drank.

And his father Isaac said unto him, Come near now, and kiss me, my son.

And he came near, and kissed him: and he smelled the smell of his raiment, and blessed him, and said, See, the smell of my son is as the smell of a field which the Lord hath blessed:

Therefore God give thee of the dew of heaven, and the fatness of the earth, and plenty of corn and wine:

Let people serve thee, and nations bow down to thee: be lord over thy brethren, and let thy mother's sons bow down to thee: cursed be every one that curseth thee, and blessed be he that blesseth thee.

(Genesis XXVII, 20 – 9)

No sooner has this blessing been delivered than Jacob departs and Esau appears, bearing his father's meal of venison and requesting his blessing. When Isaac realises that he has been deceived, he trembles with rage but refuses to bless Esau, who has now lost both his birthright and his blessing to his younger brother. Enflamed with hatred, Esau confesses to Rebecca that he is planning to slay Jacob; whereupon the boy's mother urges the latter to flee to her brother Laban, whose daughters Leah and Rachel he will eventually marry.

The subject of Isaac blessing Jacob already appears in Early Christian, Byzantine and medieval art, but it only comes into prominence in the Renaissance and seventeenth century, when it was frequently depicted by artists in both northern and southern Europe. From the earliest times, Rebecca is included in the scene of the blessing – despite the fact that the Bible does not mention her presence on this occasion – probably to identify her as the instigator of the deception. This is the case in the two most famous Renaissance treatments of the theme, Ghiberti's relief on the doors of the Baptistry in Florence of c.1439 and Raphael's fresco in the Loggia of the Vatican of 1518-19. In the latter (cf. fig. 6), an aged but vigorous Isaac raises his right arm and blesses his younger son, who is presented to him by Rebecca, who clasps Jacob in a forceful and declamatory manner which suggests that she played a decisive role in the action. Surrounding the bed of the old man is a group of anonymous figures, who serve as a chorus of onlookers, witnessing the blessing; while, at the left, Esau enters bearing the carcass of a deer, only moments too late to interrupt the blessing.

Raphael's rhetorical approach to this subject is expanded further in an undated drawing (fig. 26) by Ercole Setti (c.1530–1607), which depicts the protagonists at the right, in poses evidently inspired by the Loggia fresco. Rather than forming the focus of the composition, however, they are now displaced to one side of a large room which includes an elaborate still life, reclining dog and four servants, one of whom greets Esau as he descends a flight of stairs in a balletic pose, again bearing the carcass of a deer.

Rebecca assumes a more purely psychological role in the action in two Northern Renaissance engravings of the subject, by Martin van Heemskerck (1549) and Martin de Vos (c.1579). In the former (fig. 25), she is cast as an Old Testament prophetess, ritualistically presenting her favourite son, whose kneeling pose and cowering expression suggest his latent fear. Isaac is depicted seated and giving the blessing, his eyes staring vacantly into space. Rather than the vigorous patriarch of Raphael's work, he is now portrayed as a venerable old man, whose gestures appear stiffened with age. At the upper left, a figure who is presumably intended to be Esau enters the room. The scene is set in a domestic interior complete with a grooming dog, dozing cat and crackling fire.

Many of these features reappear in the engraving after de Vos (fig. 7), where Rebecca is accorded an even more

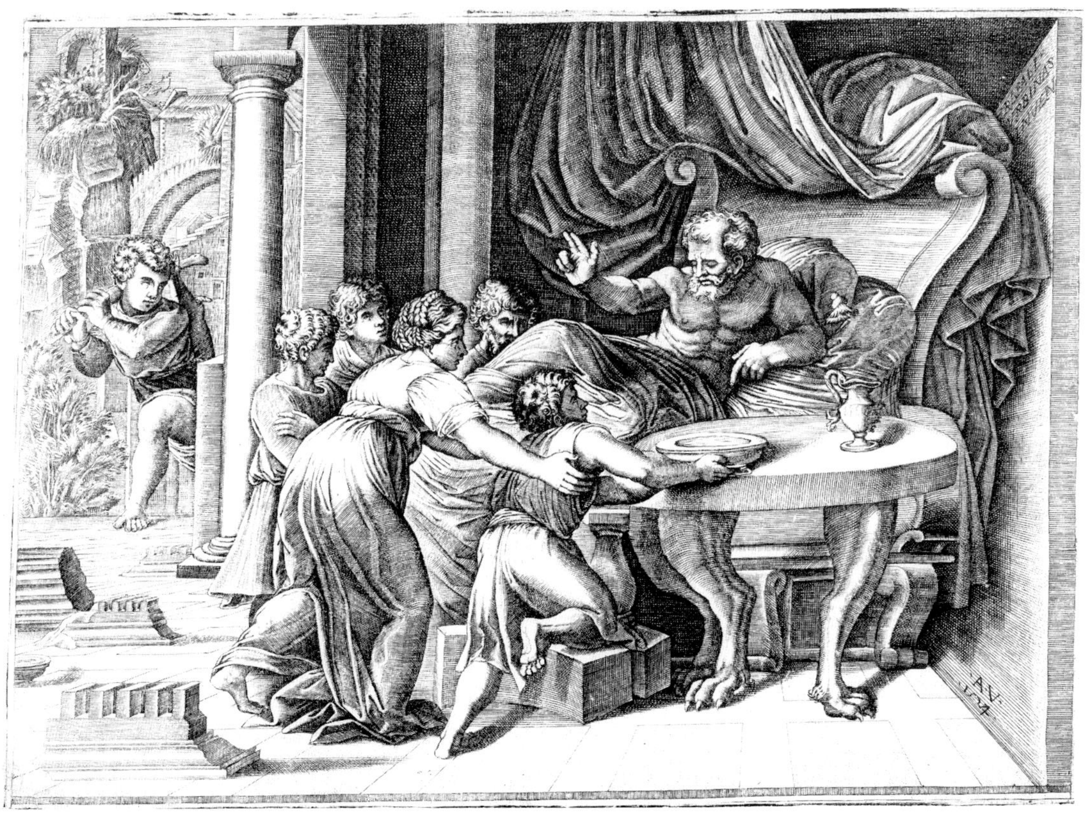

Fig. 6 (No. 13), Agostino Veneziano (after Raphael), *Isaac blessing Jacob*

passive role. It is as though she has already done her work and may now look pensively on, at its inevitable conclusion. At the right, Jacob kneels before his father in an obeisant pose, while Isaac turns to bless the youth with a tense and moderated gesture that vividly conveys his age and infirmity. Behind them, Esau enters bearing a carcass of venison and accompanied by his hunting dogs whose size and agility contrast strikingly with the sleeping lap dog in the foreground and remind us that we are witnessing an encounter between two different worlds.

The deeper, theological significance of the story becomes clear when one recalls that, from the Middle Ages onwards, the rivalry between Jacob and Esau had symbolised that between Christ and the Jews. This was the interpretation given to the tale by both Luther and Calvin, the latter of whom also regarded it as a classic example of the doctrine of predestination, citing in support of this the biblical invocation that 'the elder shall serve the younger'.[17] Viewed in this way, the role of Rebecca in the story also assumed a fundamentally

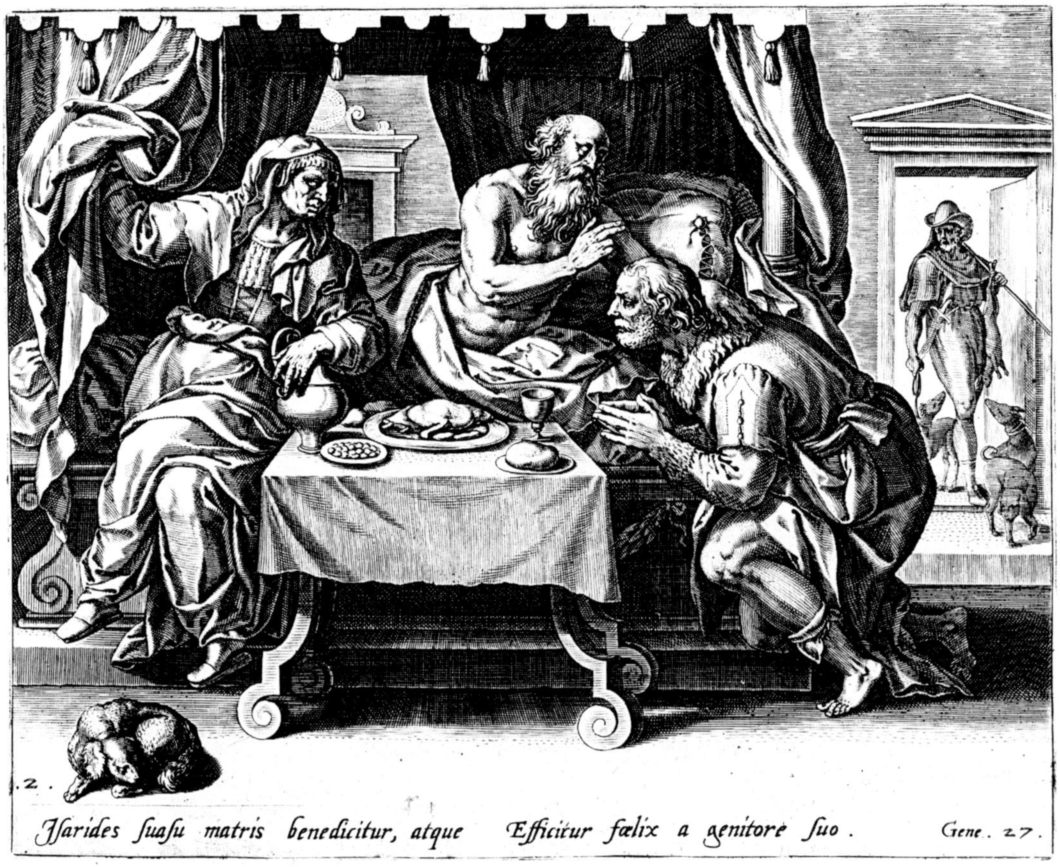

Fig. 7 (No. 16),
Martin de Vos (after),
Isaac blessing Jacob, c.1579

different purpose. Rather than being seen as a cunning wife, who deceives her aged husband, she was regarded as an agent of the Lord, whose deception 'flowed from no other source but her faith'. As Calvin observes: 'The inheritance promised by God was firmly fixed in her mind; she knew that it was decreed to her son Jacob.'[18]

This interpretation of the story, which was already endorsed by the ancient writer Josephus (AD 37/38 – 93),[19] may account for the comparatively benevolent characterisations of Rebecca found in late sixteenth century representations of the theme. In the succeeding century, however, artists were more inclined to interpret the tale on purely human terms, as one of sibling rivalry, guile and deception.

Stom's *Isaac blessing Jacob* in context

Seventeenth-century artists depicted the theme of Isaac blessing Jacob more often than those of any other age, especially in the two countries where Stom himself was active, the United Provinces and Italy. There are a number of reasons for this, the most obvious of which is the general diversification of subject matter that occurred throughout Europe in this period, evident in the art of Rubens, Poussin and many others when compared with their Renaissance predecessors. One explanation for this is the large number of illustrated Bibles produced during the preceding century, which suddenly provided artists with a wealth of new subjects that invited translation into painting. Yet another reason was the awakening of interest in themes from the Old Testament – and especially the book of Moses – among artists in the United Provinces, where the victory of the Israelites over the Egyptians was often compared with the struggles of the Dutch against their Spanish oppressors.[20] A final explanation for the upsurge of interest in the subject of Isaac blessing Jacob may be attributed to one of the most influential artists of the time, Rembrandt. Though he devoted only a handful of drawings to this subject, the great Dutch master instilled a fascination with it in any number of his pupils, who produced more than two dozen paintings and drawings of this theme in the middle years of the century.[21] This amounts to nearly half of all the depictions of the subject known from this period.

In addition to their widespread interest in the story of Isaac blessing Jacob, seventeenth-century artists also devised a radically new way of portraying it. Gone now is the full-length, long distance view of the action favoured by their predecessors, with its elaborate setting, anonymous onlookers and domestic details. In place of all these the artists of the seventeenth century adopted a more immediate and concentrated approach to the theme. With remarkable unanimity, they limited it to only the three protagonists, who are usually shown three-quarter length and at close range, filling the picture field, in direct proximity to the viewer. Typically, the space is shallow and barely defined; still-life elements are reduced to the minimum – i.e. the meal requested by Isaac; and the episode of Esau returning from the hunt is usually eliminated. Instead, Isaac's refusal to bless Esau became a separate subject for artists of the seventeenth century (cf. figs. 27 & 29). All of these innovations serve further to focus attention upon the psychological undercurrents of the action.

Two other innovations enhance the verisimilitude of these scenes: namely, the preference for realistic figures over the idealised types of the Renaissance and the prevailing emphasis upon expression, rather than gesture, in delineating the action. Virtually all of these changes derive from the influence of one artist – Caravaggio – whose dramatic, three-quarter length biblical scenes revolutionised history painting throughout much of Europe in the early seventeenth century. To him, too, may be attributed one of the most obvious transformations of the Isaac blessing Jacob theme that occurs during this

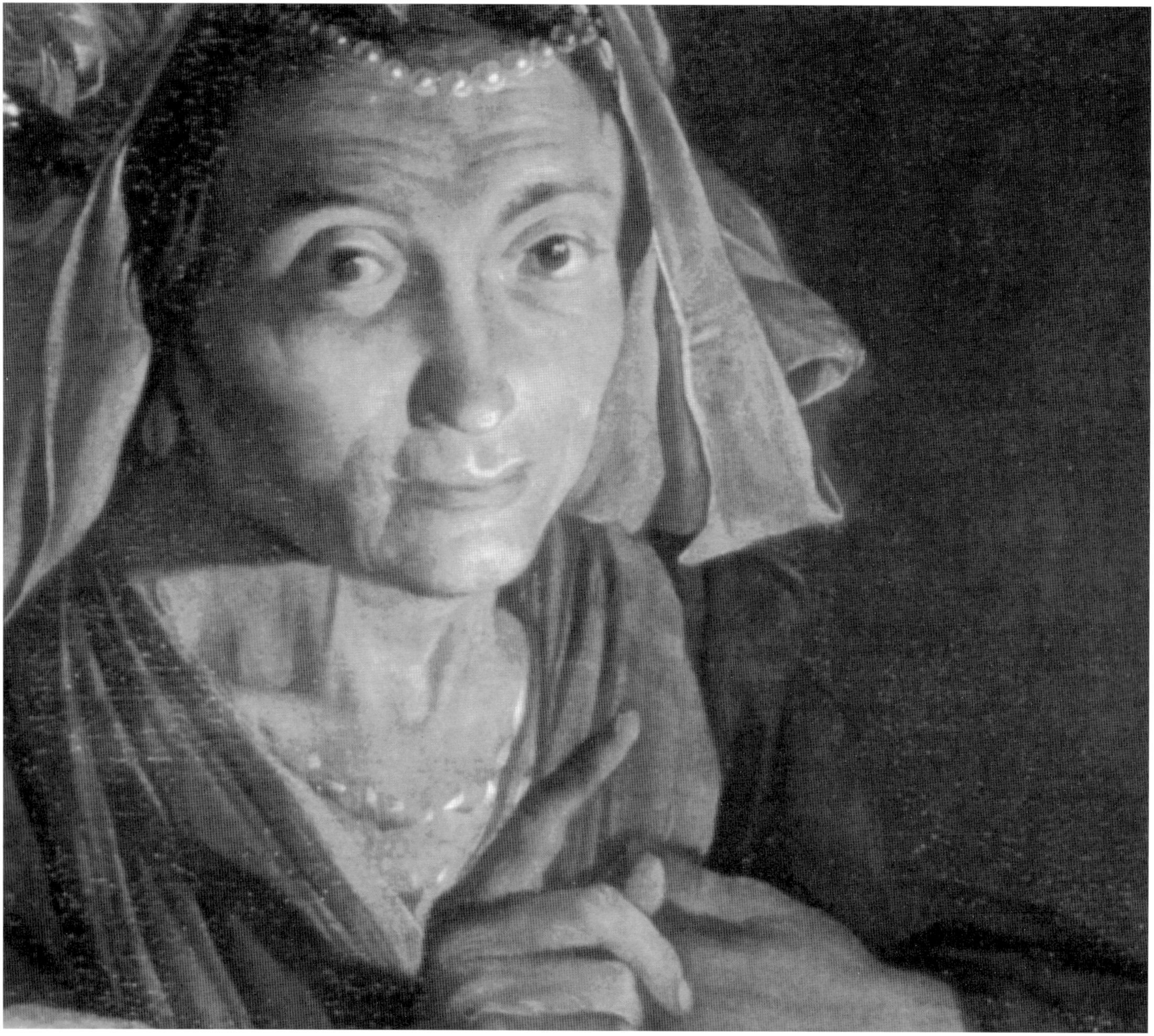

Fig. 8 (No. 1), Matthias Stom, *Isaac blessing Jacob* (detail)

period. Rather than being a mere bystander, Rebecca now becomes a more coercive and conspiratorial figure, who is psychologically implicated in the action. Though Caravaggio himself never depicted this subject, the prototype for any number of the Rebeccas which abound in seventeenth century art would appear to be in those wise and wizened crones found in such comparable works by him as *Judith and Holofernes* (Galleria Nazionale dell' Arte Antica, Rome), *Salome with the Head of John the Baptist* (National Gallery, London) or the second version of the *Supper at Emmaus* (Brera, Milan).

Stom's *Isaac blessing Jacob* (fig. 1) exemplifies this new approach to the subject and is arguably the most emotionally charged and compelling of all the painted versions of this theme. The setting consists of a bed upon which the aged Isaac reclines surrounded by Jacob and Rebecca. This is illuminated from the right by a shaft of light which floods the scene, poignantly emphasising the blind old man, who appears oblivious to it. The moment depicted is from Genesis XXVII, 21-23, and combines several stages in the action. Disconcerted with the approaching youth's voice, which is that of Jacob, Isaac has beckoned him to come closer so that he might feel his hands and assure himself that they are those of the hairy Esau. His suspicions allayed, the frail Isaac prepares to bestow the blessing. Signalling this turning point in the action are the leaping dog and the wily figure of Rebecca. Pressing her left hand to her breast, as though to proclaim her innocence, she raises her right hand in an admonishing gesture, warning the viewer not to divulge the ruse. Emerging from the shadows between the ignorant Isaac and the fearful Jacob, her scheming countenance appears to hold the entire proceedings in its sway and constitutes the emotional centre of the picture. Scarcely less well-judged is the figure of Jacob, whose trepidation is apparent in his anxious expression and divided pose, his hands moving forward with the meal while his feet appear rooted to the ground. In this ambivalent attitude, Stom summarises superbly both his eagerness to receive the blessing and his fear of detection.

Adding further to the veracity of the scene are the elaborate costumes of Jacob and Rebecca, both of whom have donned their finest dress for the occasion. Rebecca wears an elaborate headdress decorated with pearls and Jacob a red waistcoat and silver doublet tied with blue ribbons, slashed red breeches and a magnificently plumed hat. Though this display of finery provides a stunningly virtuosic pictorial flourish, it may also have been intended to impart a deeper and more ironic meaning, which throws into even sharper relief the emotional tensions of the moment. Dressed like an Old Testament prophetess, Rebecca is yet behaving like a guileful old woman, whose capacity for inflicting retribution upon the viewer appears unbounded. And dressed in 'the goodly raiment' of his elder brother, Jacob openly declares to us – if not to his father – that he is donning a disguise; for, as the Bible describes him, he 'was a plain man, dwelling in tents' (Genesis XXV, 27). Even the leaping dog may be interpreted as part of the conspiracy. Although a favourite motif of Stom's, which also appears in the *Satyr with Peasant Family* (fig. 18), it may here be intended to be impersonating one of the absent Esau's hunting dogs, thereby clinching the deception.

Though the patron of Stom's picture is unknown, it is highly likely that he was Neapolitan, since the work is traceable in that city as far back as the seventeenth century. This would provide an approximate date for the work of 1633-40. Much less mysterious is the nature of the commission of which it formed a part. Circumstantial evidence suggests that it originally formed part of a cycle of three pictures, all of which share the same provenance. These portray themes from the Old and New Testaments and the Apocrypha that involve confrontations between youth and old age. The first two of these – *Isaac blessing Jacob* and *Christ disputing with the Doctors* (figs. 1 & 2) – were executed by Stom; and the third, *Tobias healing his father's blindness* (fig. 17), was painted by an anonymous Italian artist.[22] Though the combination of these three subjects may have had some private significance for the patron, it is worth noting that Stom often produced pendants and larger sets of pictures in the course of his career, among them a group of at least a dozen works depicting episodes from the Passion of Christ (cf. fig. 20).

If the commission itself seems unusual, the order in which the pictures were intended to be seen appears somewhat less so. *Isaac blessing Jacob* and *Tobias healing his father's blindness* respectively contain three and four figures and *Christ disputing with the Doctors*, seven. The composition of the first two canvases is also closely comparable, both in the broad disposition of the figures – with the father at the right and youth(s) at the left – and in the motif of the leaping dog. This suggests that they were designed to flank *Christ disputing with the Doctors* to form a kind of narrative triptych, the theme of which is the dependence of old age upon youth either for perpetuation (Jacob), instruction (Christ) or healing (Tobias).

Though it is impossible to know what (if any) pictorial sources influenced Stom in devising this monumental treatment of the Isaac blessing Jacob theme, tantalising evidence exists that prototypes for his canvas were to be found both north and south of the Alps by the mid-1630s. Among the former was a lost painting of *Isaac blessing Jacob* by Abraham Janssens – an Antwerp master whose work Stom certainly knew – which is recorded in the inventory of the collections at Prague Castle in 1621 and then disappears from view.[23] If, as suspected, Stom journeyed to Antwerp during the 1610s, he may well have seen this canvas. Given Janssens's Italianate style and Caravaggesque leanings, it is likely to have been closely comparable to Stom's own *Isaac blessing Jacob* and may also have provided the source for the numerous depictions of this subject later produced by Jacob Jordaens (cf. fig. 30).

Even more significant for Stom's painting is the survival of two different portrayals of this theme by the Neapolitan master Filippe Vitale (1585/9-1650) and another by Francesco Guarino (1611-54).[24] Though the last of these has been dated to 1642-3, the other two are believed to have been executed around 1620. In all three, the figures are depicted half-length and pressed close to the picture plane and the setting reduced to the minimum – exactly as in Stom's painting. Where they differ markedly from the latter, however, is in the decidedly plebeian nature of the figures and costumes. But Stom's penchant for fancy dress and elaborate headgear is exactly what one would expect from an artist influenced by the Utrecht Caravaggisti, who repeatedly portrayed such exotically clad figures.

In the absence of an exact date for the Barber Institute's painting, it is unclear what relationship it bears to the most celebrated depiction of *Isaac blessing Jacob* executed in Naples during these years. This is Ribera's canvas of 1637 (fig. 9), painted for an unidentified patron and, judging by its unusual format, probably intended as an overdoor.[25] In this, Isaac is shown feeling Jacob's hands as Rebecca nudges the boy forward. Gazing out of the picture and wearing a somewhat disingenuous expression – as if to assert her innocence – she points with her left hand to the scene of the blessing, confusingly confessing to her involvement in the deception. At the far left, Esau appears in a doorway, returning from the hunt – one of his rare appearances in a seventeenth century painting of this theme.

Ribera's canvas possesses the dextrous handling, lustrous chromaticism and masterly description of textures typical of his vigorous and earthy style. This is especially apparent in the brilliant depiction of the drapery and still-life, executed with a fluency and vitality that transcend the constraints of Stom's more orthodox technique. But the great Spanish master does not necessarily surpass his rival in his exploration of the mystery and intrigue that are implicit in the theme; and it is noteworthy that, whichever canvas was painted first, the two bear no relationship to one another in conception,

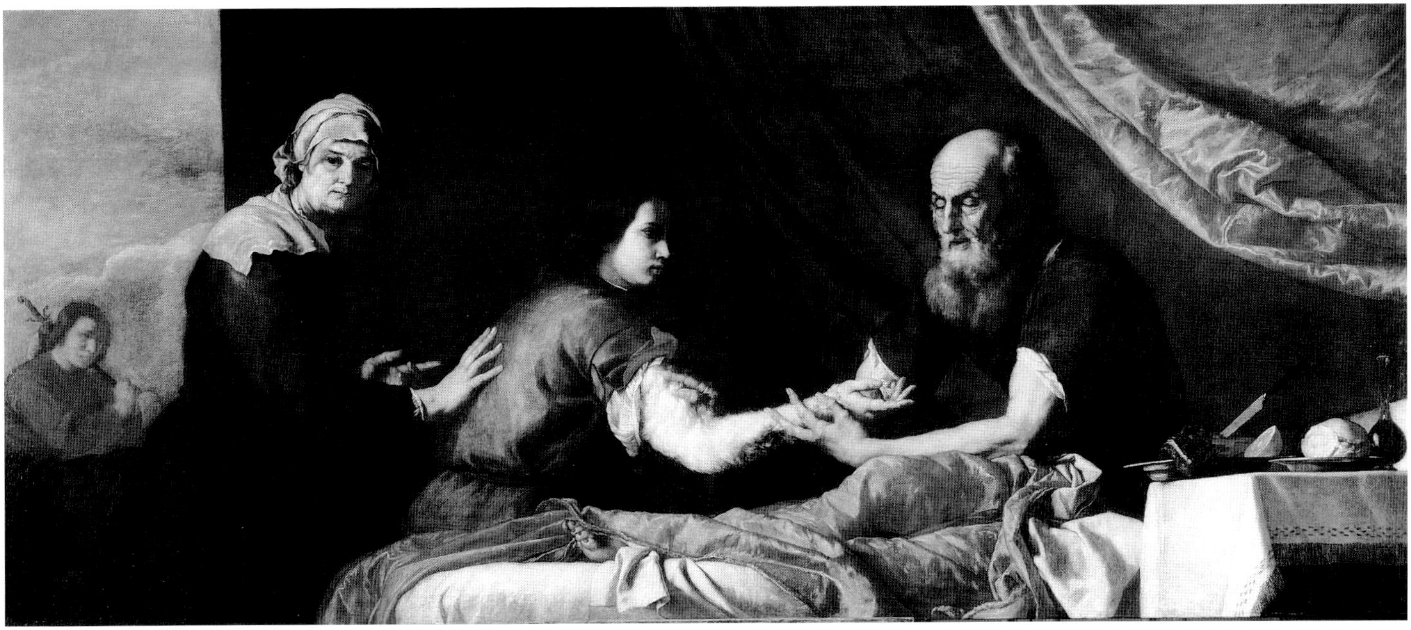

Fig. 9, Jusepe de Ribera, *Isaac blessing Jacob*, 1637, Museo del Prado, Madrid

indicating that they are entirely independent works. For one, the moment chosen by Ribera is more straightforward – even matter-of-fact – in its depiction of Isaac and Jacob and illustrates just three short words ('he felt him') from Genesis XXVII, 22. Though Isaac is blinded, there is no evidence that he is incredulous; and, though Jacob is plainly disguised, there is no indication that he is fearful. An even greater divide separates the two works when one turns to the figure of Rebecca. Not only is she less strategically positioned in relation to her husband and son in Ribera's picture, but her expression appears much less furtive and scheming. Moreover, if Stom's old woman poses a potential threat to the viewer, Ribera's functions merely as an intermediary, drawing our attention to the blessing scene between father and son.

The psychological complexity of Stom's canvas finds its closest counterparts not in paintings produced in Italy during these years but in those encountered in Dutch art, especially works emanating from the school of Rembrandt. Since all of these date from the 1630s or later, there can be little question of any direct influence; though the similarities again raise the nagging question of a common source in Dutch or Flemish art of the 1610s or '20s, such as the lost painting by Janssens already mentioned. The existence of an *Isaac and Esau* (cf. fig. 27) of c. 1628 by Jan Lievens, who was a close associate of Rembrandt in Leiden in the late 1620s, attests to an early interest in the subject among artists connected with the great Dutch master. But those works which invite direct comparison with Stom's picture all date from the following decade, when Rembrandt had settled in Amsterdam.

The masterpiece of this group in Govaert Flinck's *Isaac blessing Jacob* (fig. 10) of 1638, which is one of two canvases on this subject by Rembrandt's most gifted pupil of the 1630s. In this, both the position of the bed and the arrangement of the figures present obvious similarities

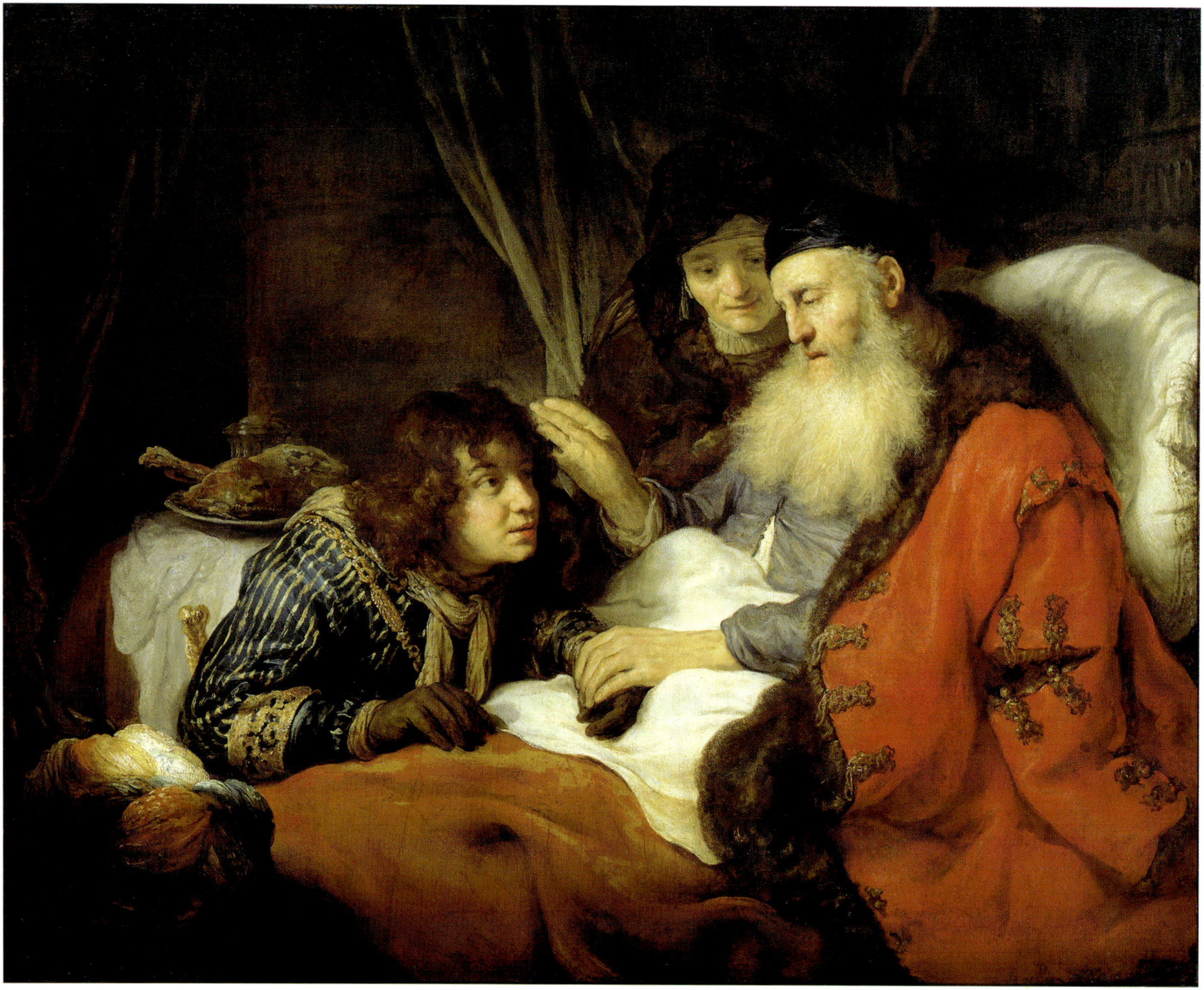

Fig. 10 (No. 10), Govaert Flinck, *Isaac blessing Jacob*, 1638, Rijksmuseum, Amsterdam

with Stom's composition, though the figures are presented half-length and in even closer proximity to the viewer. The moment depicted is that of the paternal blessing. Isaac has just felt Jacob's gloved left hand and, convinced that he is the hairy Esau, blesses him. Between the two, Rebecca gazes warily on, in silent anticipation of the success of the plot. In the frail figure of Isaac and the eager and expectant expression of Jacob, Flinck imbues the scene with a tenderness and humanity that bespeak a pupil of Rembrandt. But the work lacks the nervous tension and emotional divisiveness of Stom's more highly charged scene, which remains the only canvas of this subject in which the viewer is directly insinuated into the action through the admonishing figure of Rebecca.

The comparison with Flinck's painting also serves to emphasise the somewhat hybrid nature of Stom's style – in short, its mixture of Dutch and Italianate elements. Among the former are the detailed interest in costume – a joint legacy of the Utrecht Caravaggisti – and the incisively delineated expressions of the figures. But Stom eschews the more purely domestic elements of Flinck's painting, e.g. the still-life of the meal laid out on a table at the rear and the meticulous description of the pillow and bedding. Nor does he present us with the pathetic and richly clad Isaac of Flinck's canvas. Instead, we have an 'heroically' nude Isaac surrounded by mere drapery rather than bedding, together with a plain black background. All of these features ultimately derive from Caravaggio and serve to elevate the story to a more timeless and symbolic realm.

Flinck's painting serves as a reminder of the broad similarities between Stom's picture and those produced by numerous other artists of the Rembrandt school. But these – and Rembrandt's own drawings of the subject (cf. fig. 28) – all date from later than Stom's *Isaac blessing Jacob* and are irrelevant to an account of its artistic context. For the final chapter of this story, one must return instead to the artist's adopted homeland, Italy.

The dominant figure in Neapolitan painting of the late seventeenth century was the immensely prolific Luca Giordano (1632–1705), who modelled his earliest works on those of Ribera and his contemporaries to be seen in the city. One of these is a canvas of *Isaac blessing Jacob* (fig. 11) which is datable to the early 1650s. Giordano was clearly familiar with Ribera's celebrated painting of this theme, which provides the obvious source for the pose and disguised arms of Jacob and the ignoble features of Rebecca, who is here shown skulking behind Jacob, as though momentarily forgetting that her husband is blind. The style of the work, too, is closely modelled on the broad and thickly textured handling of the great Spanish master. The source for the pathetic figure of Isaac, however, is not in Ribera but in the Barber Institute's Stom, which likewise inspired the motif of the bed and overhanging drape and the stark black background. To be sure, there are significant differences between the two, even in the figure of Isaac. In Giordano's canvas he appears as a more muscular and Italianate figure, who is posed relaxedly and (due to Jacob's proximity) need not strain to deliver the blessing. In Stom's painting, he is portrayed instead as a gaunt and wasting figure who gropes poignantly into space, seeking to establish contact with his son. But these differences cannot disguise the fact that Giordano created his *Isaac blessing Jacob* in direct emulation of the two greatest works on the theme to be seen in Naples, one by Ribera and the other by Stom.

Matthias Stom is so elusive – even invisible – a figure in the annals of the history of art that attempting to reconstruct his career is itself a form of groping in the dark. Unsurprisingly, then, the whole question of his influence upon his contemporaries remains even more unfathomable. But influence he certainly wielded, even upon the young and impressionable Giordano, whose *Isaac blessing Jacob* has one other striking similarity to the Barber Institute's Stom: namely, that the two paintings are virtually identical in size. This is unlikely to be a

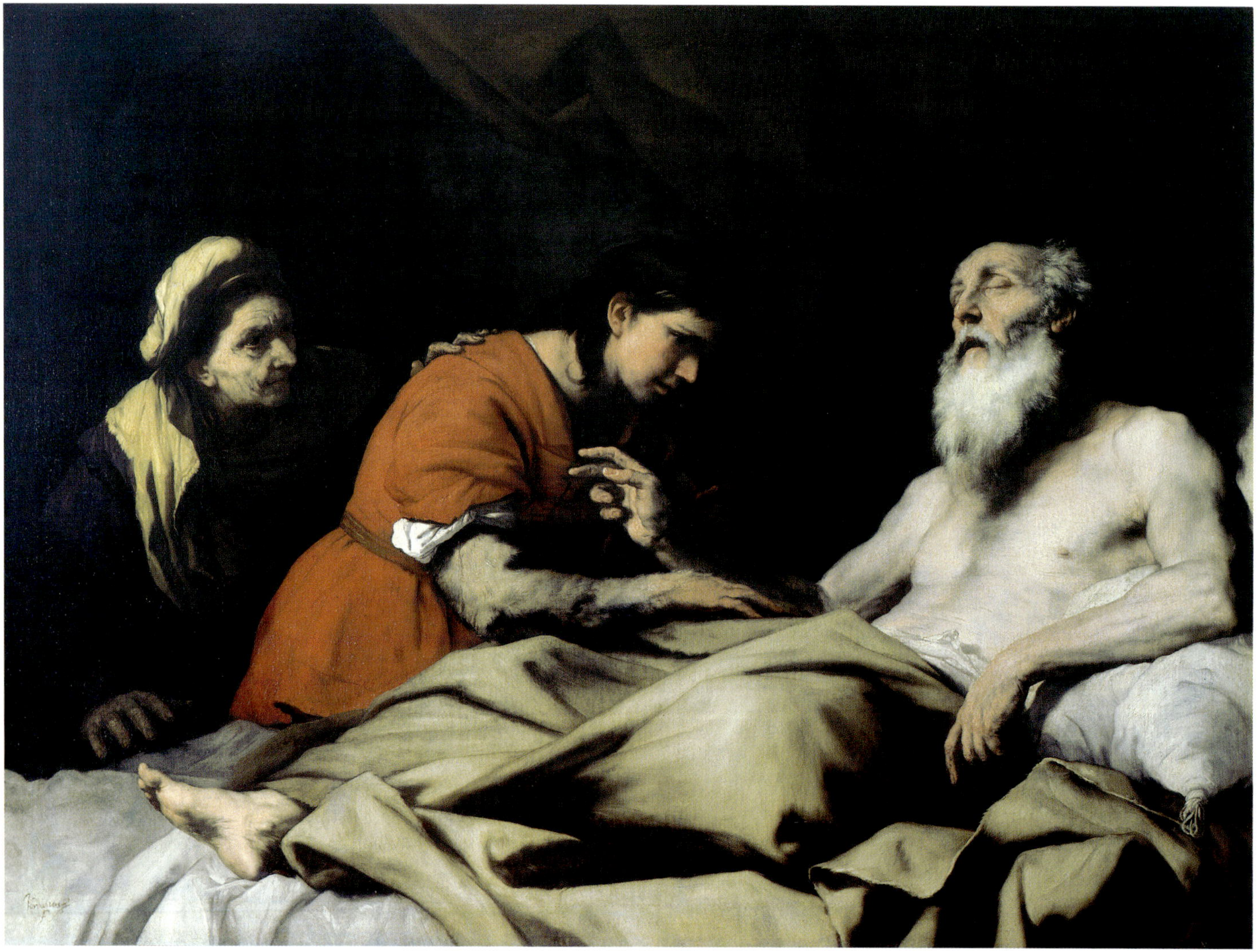

Fig. 11 (No. 11), Luca Giordano, *Isaac blessing Jacob*,
Count Harrach Family Collection, Schloss Rohrau, Lower Austria

coincidence and prompts one to wonder if Giordano was commissioned to paint an identically sized variant of Stom's canvas by a patron who particularly admired the latter but could not own it. As with so much else in the case of Stom, the question will remain forever unanswered.

Surprising as it is to discover this connection between an itinerant Dutch master whose reputation entered oblivion after his death and one of the most celebrated of all Italian baroque painters, it is even more extraordinary to discover that Stom's Caravaggesque works were already known and admired during his own lifetime at the opposite end of Europe, in England.

A note on Stom and England

Though the art of Caravaggio and his Dutch followers was well-known at the court of Charles I, who acquired the former's great *Death of the Virgin* (Louvre, Paris) from the Duke of Mantua's collection in 1627, Caravaggism exerted no influence upon developments in British art until the eighteenth century. The exception that proves this rule is the only Caravaggesque painting known to have been executed in England before this: namely, the copy of Stom's *Salome receiving the Head of John the Baptist* (figs. 12 & 13) by William Dobson (1611-46), the greatest native-born English artist of the seventeenth century. Anomalous though this work is, it was much celebrated. According to Gambarini, it was regarded as Dobson's most important history picture – an opinion also endorsed by Sir Peter Lely – and Dobson himself refused to part with it during his lifetime.[26] The picture was itself copied by another English master of the period, Isaac Fuller (?1606-72), though this no longer survives. All of these artists and critics presumably regarded the composition as Dobson's original invention. The painting was also commended by Walpole and, later, Waagen, who noted that Dobson 'here appears in conception and effect to have taken Gerard Honthorst for his model'[27] – a misattribution which is understandable, coming at a time when Stom's identity was unknown. But the highest accolade paid to it was John Dean's mezzotint after the composition of 1786 (fig. 32), which was also particularly timely. For it coincided exactly with the career of Joseph Wright of Derby (1734-97), the only British painter of the first rank to have based his style on that of Caravaggio and his followers (cf. fig. 33).

Dobson's copy differs in certain details from Stom's original, which depicts Salome wearing different jewellery and given a more idealised facial type. The flame of the candle held by the boy also appears more naturalistic in the copy and the handling of the picture more agitated and painterly. But the chief difference is the inclusion of the executioner's right arm in the original. Since the vertical dimensions of both canvases are nearly identical and the width of the Dobson some 25 cm shorter than the original, it seems likely that the copy has been cropped at the left and that the two works were originally the same size.

A more intriguing question is how Dobson actually knew the Stom and the possible implications this might have upon the likely date of the original. Since Dobson never went abroad, it must be assumed that Stom's canvas was in England by c.1640, the approximate date of Dobson's copy. But had it come here from Rome or Naples or only from Northern Europe? On stylistic grounds, it is consistent with the group of paintings that appear to be the artist's earliest Caravaggesque works, in its flowing and voluminous draperies and idealised facial types. This makes it possible – though by no means certain – that it was painted in Utrecht or Antwerp around 1625, before Stom set out for Italy, and imported into England sometime after. When one considers that Honthorst was invited to work at the court of Charles I in 1628, and that two works by him could also be seen in the Duke of Buckingham's collection, the arrival of yet another Caravaggesque painting on these shores at this

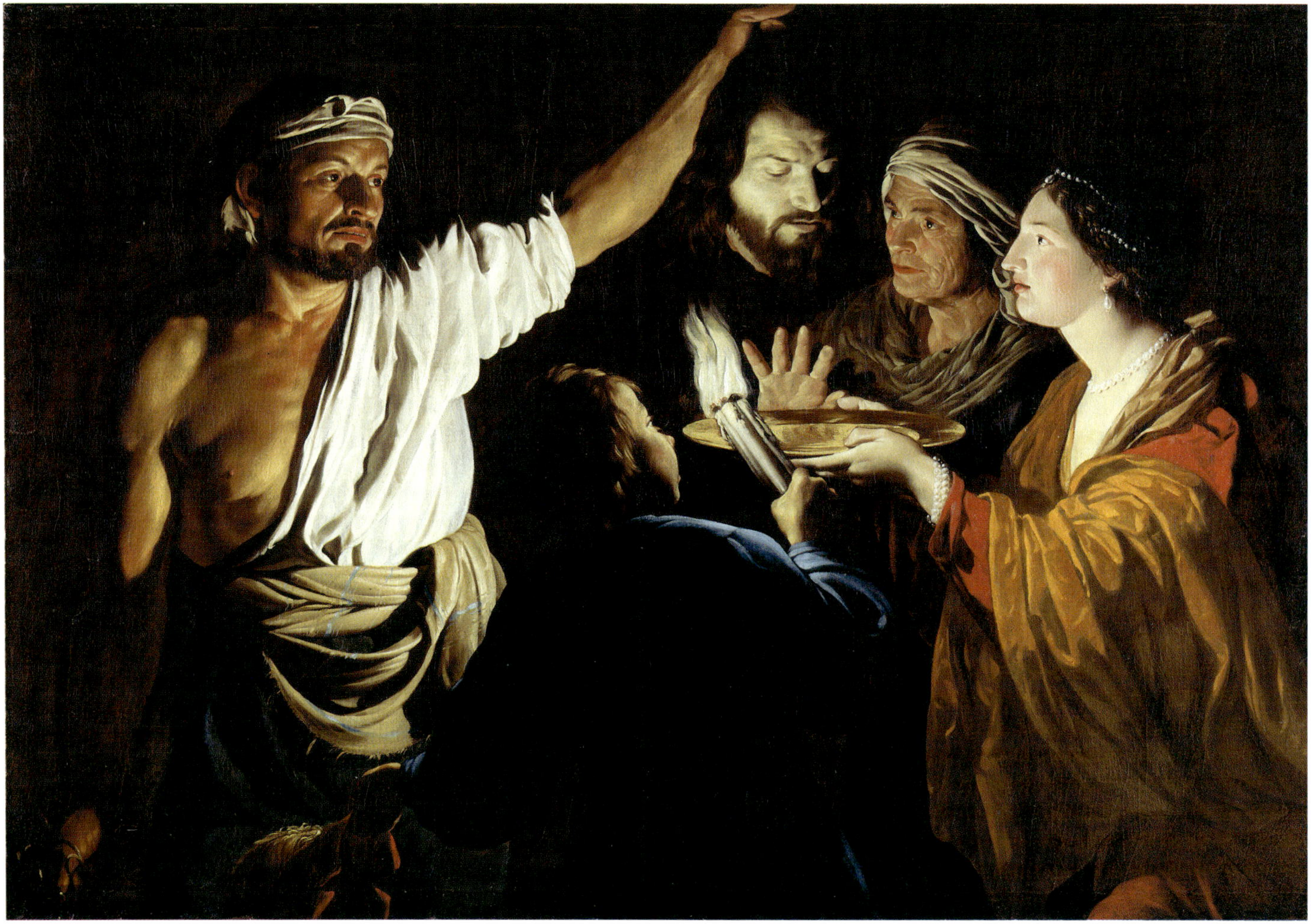

Fig. 12 (No. 5), Matthias Stom, *Salome receiving the Head of John the Baptist*, Collection of Sir Denis Mahon

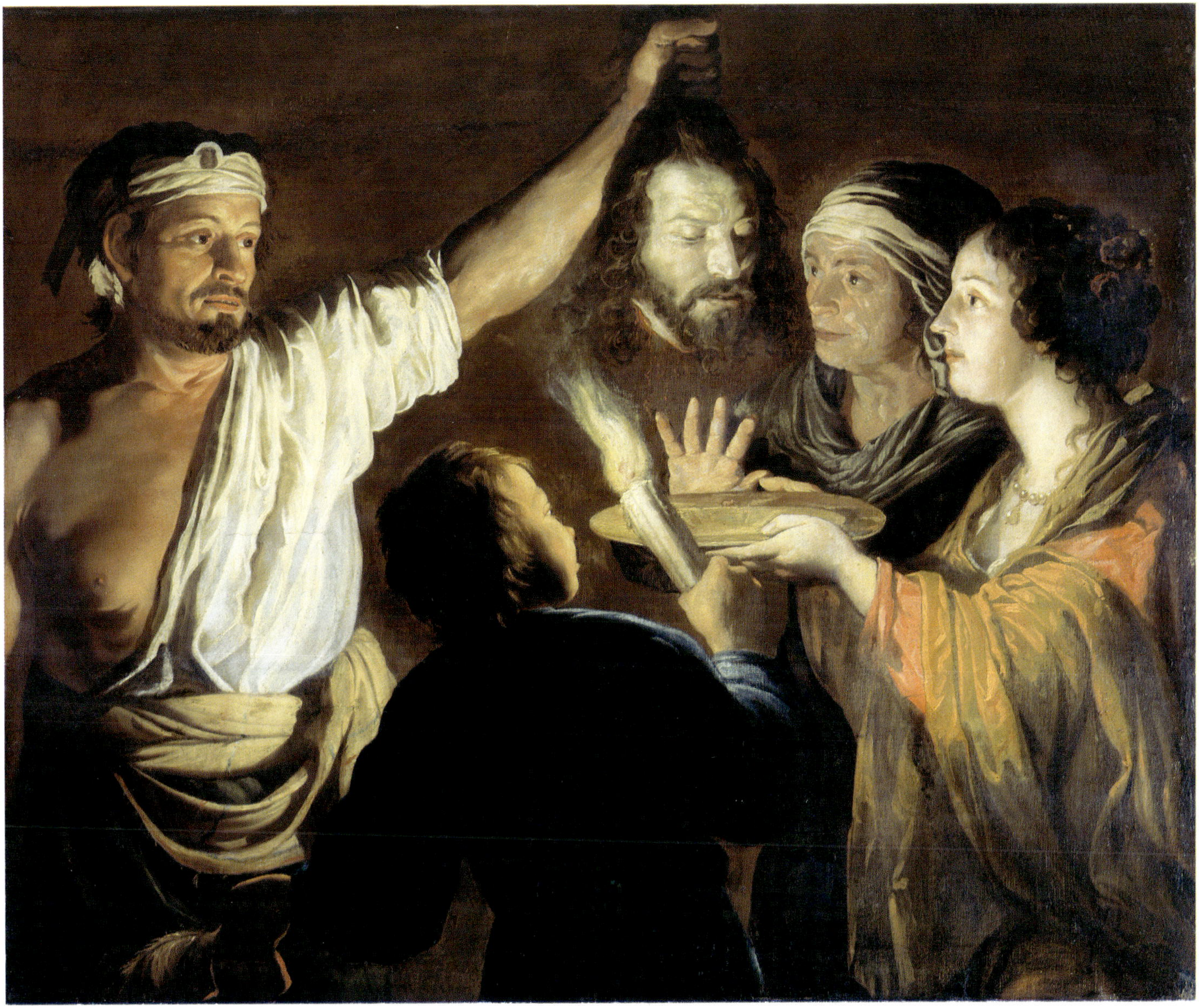

Fig. 13 (No. 12), William Dobson (after Stom), *Salome receiving the Head of John the Baptist*, Walker Art Gallery, Liverpool

moment does not seem so surprising. What one would really wish to know, however, was what it arrived *as* – a work by the ubiquitous Honthorst or by the fledgling Matthias Stom?

One other tantalising piece of evidence exists that paintings by Stom were known in England (by whatever name) at a comparatively early date. In c.1656 a 'Nightpiece of A man A drinking' was inventoried in the collection of Ralph Bankes at Gray's Inn, London. This is the *Man with a Glass of Wine, Pipe and Fiddle* (fig. 4) now preserved in the Bankes Family Collection at Kingston Lacy. Though the picture remained unattributed in early inventories of the collection, in 1762 it was ascribed to Frans Hals. More recent inventories have attributed it to Gerard Seghers (cf. fig. 31) and Honthorst himself. Only in 1979 was it eventually given to Stom. This confusing and unhappy fate serves to underscore what students of the artist have always known about Stom: namely, that his works were more famous than his name.

1 G. J. Hoogewerff, *Nederlandsche Kunstenaars te Rome (1600-1725)*, The Hague, 1942, p. 279.
2 C. Celano, *Delle Notizie del Bello, dell'Antico e del Curioso della Città di Napoli*, Naples, 1692, part VII, p. 29.
3 Vincenzo Ruffo, 'Galleria Ruffo nel secolo XVII in Messina: I', *Bolletino d'Arte*, 1916, pp. 29 and 32.
4 *Il Seicento a Bergamo*, Palazzo Ragione, Bergamo, 1987, p. 203, no. 52.
5 Cf. Rodolfo Palluchini, *La Pittura Veneziana del Seicento*, Milan, 1981, p. 323.
6 Celano, *op. cit.*, p. 29.
7 Nicolson (1977, p. 230) states that he is described as a pupil of Honthorst in the Ruffo inventory cited in note 3 above, but this is incorrect. The source of this error is G. J. Hoogewerff ('Rembrandt en een Italiaansche Maecenas,' *Oud Holland*, 1917, p. 132).
8 The most complete list of these is provided by Nicolson, 1989, pp. 179-88. See also pp. 65–7 below.
9 Ruffo, *op. cit.*, pp. 29 and 32.
10 For which, see the list of abbreviated texts on p. 9 above.
11 Nicolson, 1977, p. 230.
12 The key works in this group (with Nicolson 1989, cat. nos.) are *St Sebastian tended by Irene* (1460), *Tobias and the Angel* (1471), *Lot's Flight from Sodom* (1472), *The Adoration of the Magi* (1473), *The Annunciation* (1474), *The Adoration of the Shepherds* (1515), *Sarah brings Hagar to Abraham* (1559) and the *Angel and Virgin of Annunciation* (1560 a, b).
13 As Nicolson (1977, p. 240) observed, Rubens's *Judith and Holofernes* (Herzog Anton Ulrich-Museum, Braunschweig) of 1617 and *Old Woman with a Brazier* (Gemäldegalerie Alte Meister, Dresden) of 1616-17 directly anticipate the artificial light effects and fiery colouring of Stom's mature works. Stom also appears to have found inspiration in Rubens's *Prometheus* (Philadelphia Museum of Art) of 1610-11 and *Lot and his Daughters fleeing Sodom* (Louvre, Paris) of 1625 when devising his own versions of these themes (Nicolson 1989, nos. 1472 & 1506). The exaggerated musculature and deeply weathered skin encountered in Stom may also be seen in certain works by Abraham Janssens, among them *Philomen and Baucis* (Wellesley College Museum, Massachusetts) of 1615-20 and *St Jerome* (four versions known; one exh. *Portraits and Figures in Painting and Sculpture 1570-1870*, 15 June – 26 August 1983, Heim Gallery, London, no. 3). Jordaens's paintings of the Holy Family and the Adoration of the Shepherds of c. 1616 were also almost certainly known to Stom, who borrowed the motif of a leaping dog from a version of the latter theme in the Antwerp Museum and repeated it *ad nauseam* throughout his career, including the Barber Institute's *Isaac blessing Jacob*. As Nicolson (1977, p. 239) observed, Stom also appears to have based the facial type of his *Soldier lighting a candle from an oil lamp* (Nicolson, 1989, no. 1484) upon the figure of Joseph in Jordaens's *Holy Family with Shepherds* (Metropolitan Museum of Art, New York) of 1616 and modelled the figure of a

man holding a rope in his *Capture of Christ* (Nicolson, 1989, no. 1463) at Ottawa on the maidservant masking a candle in Jordaens's *Holy Family* in the Nationalmuseum, Stockholm.

14 The two pictures that signal this conversion are Bloemaert's *Fluteplayer* of 1621 (Centraal Museum, Utrecht) and *Supper at Emmaus* of 1622 (Musées Royaux des Beaux-Arts de Belgique, Brussels); for which, see Marcel G. Roethlisberger, *Abraham Bloemaert and his Sons*, Doornspijk, 1993, I, pp. 220-3, nos. 284-5.

15 The other major Caravaggesque artist of these years who specialised in candlelight scenes was Trophime Bigot (1579-1650), who was in Rome from 1620 to 1629 (and conceivably until 1634) and whose works have occasionally been confused with Stom's (cf. Nicolson, 1977, p. 240). Both artists were much influenced by Honthorst and, given the close similarities between their works, must have known one another in Rome.

16 Nicolson, 1977, p. 234. One other characteristic of Stom's Sicilian patrons is that some of them were apparently also very learned; for, of the more than half dozen scenes from ancient history that may be attributed to the artist, the majority have a Sicilian provenance and are executed on a vast scale.

17 John Calvin, *Commentaries on the First Book of Moses called Genesis*, trns. the Rev. John King M.A., Edinburgh, 1850, II, pp. 81-103. Luther's interpretation of the story, which is essentially the same, is recounted fully in *Luther's Works*, Volume 5, Lectures on Genesis Chapters 26-30, ed. Jaroslav Pelikan, Saint Louis, 1968, pp. 99-187.

18 Calvin, *op. cit.*, pp. 84-5.

19 Josephus, *Complete Works*, trns. William Whiston, Grand Rapids, Michigan, 1981, pp. 39-40.

20 For the importance of this theme in Dutch art of the period, see especially: *Im Lichte Rembrandts, Das Alte Testament im Goldenen Zeitalter der Niederländischen Kunst*, Westfälisches Landesmuseum, Münster, 1994, pp. 37-9.

21 For the relevant paintings, see: Werner Sumowski, *Gemälde der Rembrandt-Schüler*, Landau/Pfalz, 1983, Vols. II, p. 726, no. 397 (G. van den Eeckhout); p. 1019, nos. 613-14 (Flinck); p. 1390, nos. 907-9 (Horst); III, p. 1486, no. 971 (Kneller); IV, p. 2602, no. 1746; p. 2607, no. 1769; and p. 2610, no. 1782 (Victors); VI, p. 3745, no. 2454 (Verelst); p. 3705, no. 2261a (A. van Dijck). For the drawings, see: Werner Sumowski, *Drawings of the Rembrandt School*, New York, 1979-92, Vols. I, p. 422, no. 199x (Bol); IV, p. 1886, no. 862 and p. 1974, no. 905ax (Flinck); V, p. 2408, no. 1081xx (A. de Gelder); p. 2518, no. 1132x; p. 2558, no. 1151x; and p. 2700, no. 1218x (S. van Hoogstraten); VII, p. 3896, no. 1753xx (Lievens); VIII, p. 3976, no. 1767, and p. 4274, no. 1910x (Maes). Cf. also fig. 29 below. For drawings by (or attributed to) Rembrandt on this theme, see: Otto Benesch, *The Drawings of Rembrandt*, London, 1973, I, p. 38, no. 134; III, p. 140, nos. 507-10; V, p. 250, nos. 891-2 and p. 292, no. 1065.

22 For a full bibliography on the three pictures in this cycle, see cat. nos. 1 and 2 below.

23 Heinrich Zimmerman, 'Das Inventar der Prager Schatz– und Kunstkammer vom 6. Dezember 1621', *Jahrbuch der Kunsthistorischen Sammlungen des Allerhöchsten Kaiserhauses*, XXV, 1905, p. XLIV, no. 1141.

24 Cf. *Civiltà del Seicento a Napoli*, Museo di Capodimonte, Naples, 1984, pp. 328-9 (Guarino); *Battistello Caracciolo e il primo naturalismo a Napoli*, Castel Sant'Elmo, Naples, 1991, pp. 110 and 136 (Vitale), 139 (copy after Guarino).

25 For a recent discussion of this picture, plus further bibliography, see: Alfonso E. Pérez Sanchez and Nicola Spinosa, *Jusepe de Ribera 1591-1652*, The Metropolitan Museum of Art, New York, 1992, pp. 123-6.

26 C. Gambarini, *Description of the Earl of Pembroke's Pictures*, 1731, pp. IX, 79.

27 G. F. Waagen, *Treasures of Art in Great Britain*, London, 1854, III, p. 154.

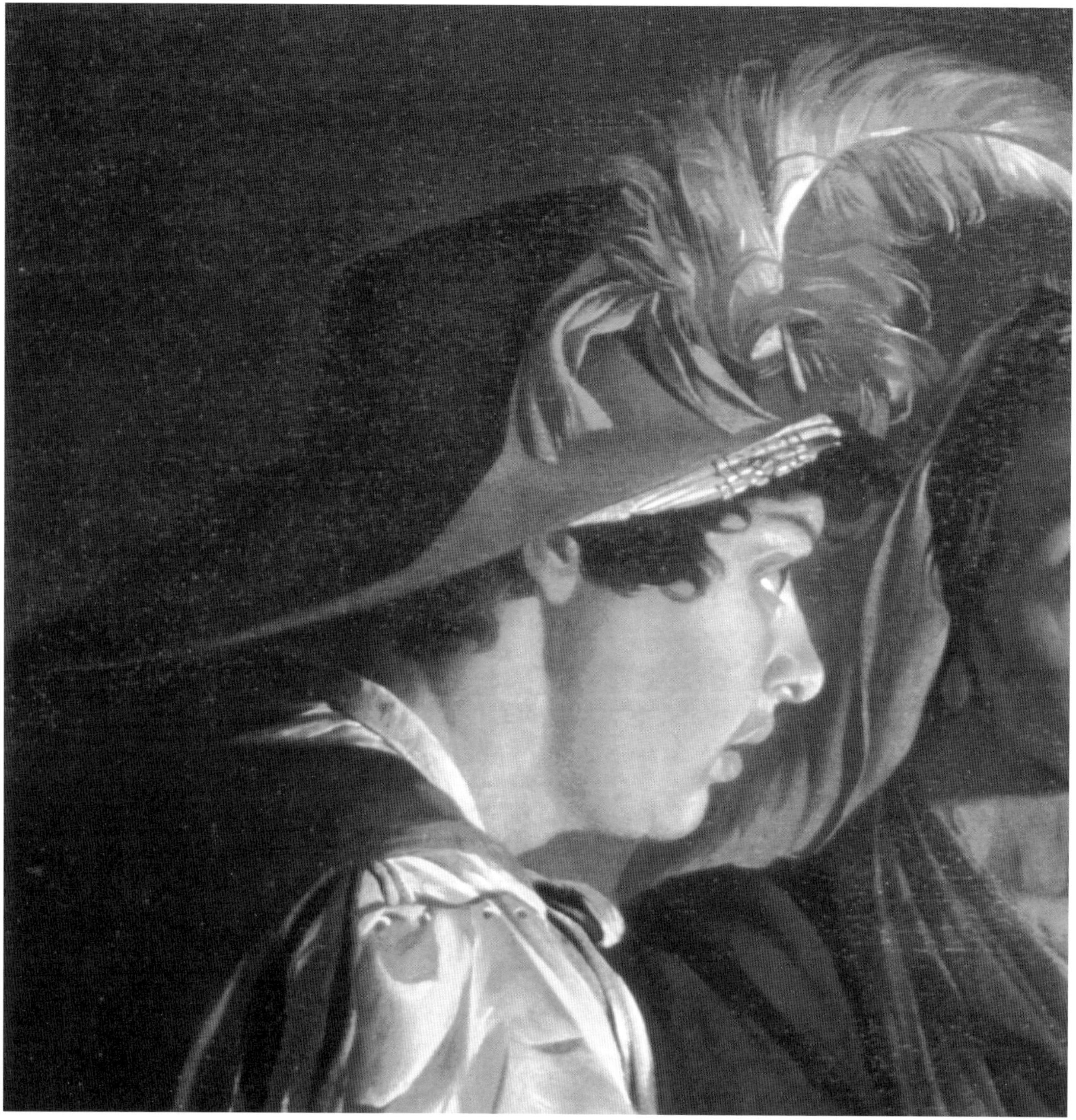

Fig. 14 (No. 1), Matthias Stom, *Isaac blessing Jacob* (detail)

CATALOGUE

Matthias Stom (c. 1600 –? after 1652)

1 **Isaac blessing Jacob**, c. 1633 – 40
[Fig. 1, p. 10]

Oil on canvas, 136.5 x 182 cm.

The Barber Institute of Fine Arts, The University of Birmingham

Isaac blessing Jacob is one of three paintings commissioned by an unknown patron, almost certainly in Naples, in the late 1630s. The other members of the cycle are *Christ disputing with the Doctors* (fig. 2), also by Stom, and *Tobias healing his father's blindness* (fig. 17), which was executed by an unidentified Italian artist who was evidently a collaborator of Stom.[1] The theme linking the cycle is the confrontation between youth and old age in the Old and New Testaments and the Apocrypha. This unusual programme may have had some private significance for the patron.

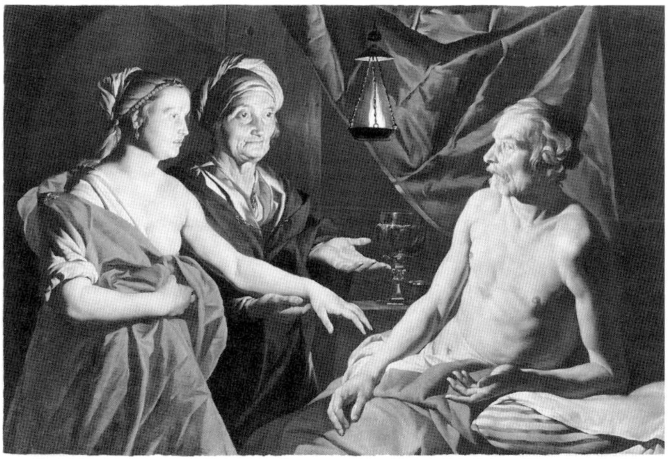

Fig. 15, Matthias Stom, *Sarah bringing Hagar to Abraham*, Staatliche Museen zu Berlin, Gemäldegalerie

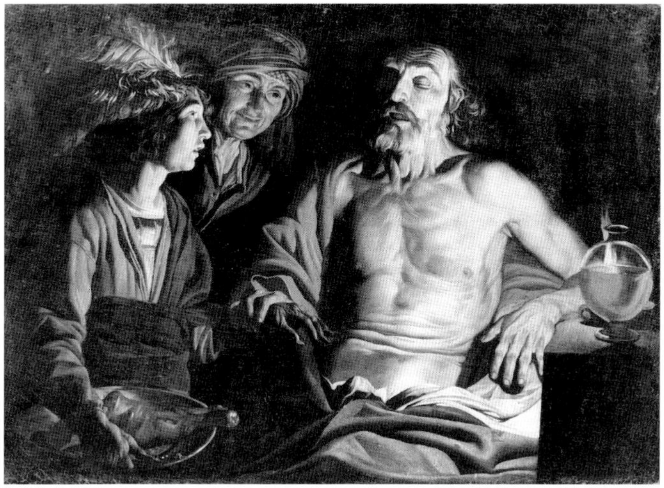

Fig. 16, Follower of Matthias Stom, *Isaac blessing Jacob*, Musée du Louvre, Paris

In this picture, Stom depicts a subject from Genesis XXVII, 1–29. The aged Isaac, nearly blind, has summoned his favourite son Esau to prepare a meal and receive the paternal blessing. Instead, Rebecca – Isaac's wife – substitutes her own favourite son, Jacob, dressing him up in goat skin gloves so that he will resemble his hairy brother. The tension and duplicity of the moment are brilliantly captured by Stom in the fearful pose and expression of Jacob, who proffers the meal while hesitating to step forward, and in the artful countenance of Rebecca, who raises her right hand to warn the viewer not to divulge the plot.

The picture also contains references to the Five Senses: sight (through its absence in Isaac), touch (the blessing), hearing (again through its opposite, i.e. the silence demanded by Rebecca), taste (the meal), and smell (the leaping dog). The last of these is a recurrent motif of Stom's (cf. fig. 18), which may derive from Jacob Jordaens's *Adoration of the Shepherds* of c.1616 in the Antwerp Museum, a picture that Stom could have known.

The design of the present picture is closely comparable to that of Stom's *Sarah bringing Hagar to Abraham* (fig. 15), which treats a theme from Genesis XVI, 1 – 3. Though it is impossible to determine which picture was painted first, the relationship between the two is characteristic of Stom, who often employed similar compositions when portraying very different subjects.

Another version of *Isaac blessing Jacob* (fig. 16) attributed to Stom is in the Louvre. Until the emergence of the present picture, it was regarded as a copy of a lost original. Now it is considered to be by an anonymous follower of the artist and provides telling evidence that the elusive Stom attracted imitators. Despite the widespread popularity of the subject in seventeenth-century Europe, the two paintings are among the rare depictions of Isaac blessing Jacob by a Caravaggesque painter.

For a fuller discussion of the Barber Institute's picture in context, see the introductory essay to this catalogue, pp. 23–31.

1 For the history and bibliography of this cycle, see p. 39, note 1.

Reference: *Trafalgar Galleries at the Royal Academy IV*, London, 1985, pp. 16–19, no. 4.

2 Christ disputing with the Doctors, c.1633–40 [Fig. 2, p. 11]

Oil on canvas, 136 x 181 cm.

Collection of Mr. A. Alfred Taubman

This is one of three paintings that formed a cycle commissioned by an unidentified Neapolitan patron, probably between 1633 and 1640, when Stom resided in the city. Its pendants were *Isaac blessing Jacob* (fig. 1) by Stom and *Tobias healing his father's blindness* (fig. 17) by an anonymous Italian artist who has tentatively been identified as Paolo Finoglia (c.1590–1656).[1] The three paintings originally formed a type of devotional 'triptych' portraying subjects involving confrontations between youth and old age from the Old and New Testaments and the Apocrypha.

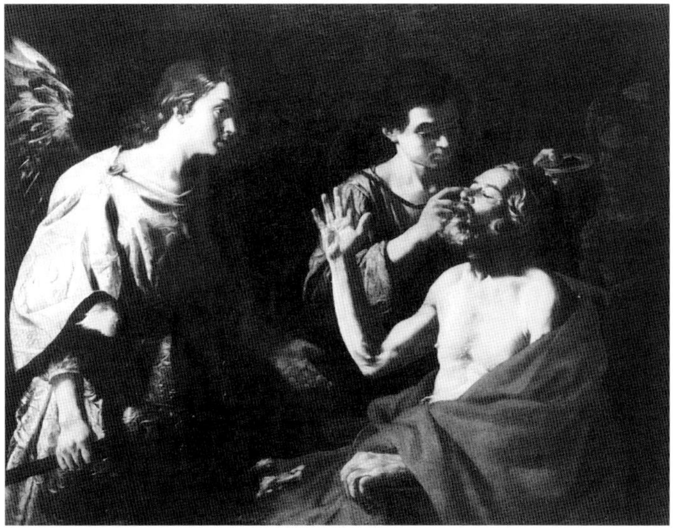

Fig. 17, Anonymous Italian, *Tobias healing his father's blindness*, Private Collection

The subject of this picture is from Luke II, 42 – 52. The twelve-year-old Christ has escaped from his parents and entered Solomon's Temple in Jerusalem, where he discourses with a group of Jewish scribes who 'were astonished by his understanding and answers'. With his right hand raised, in the exact centre of the picture, Christ is shown preaching surrounded by six elders, three of whom hold massive tomes, symbolising the Old Law. In the quizzical expression of the seated man at the left, Stom vividly conveys their questioning nature. This is intensified by the compact grouping of all the figures around Christ, which suggests a close and heated debate.

The style of the picture is characteristic of Stom's art at its most eye-catching and self-assured. This is especially apparent in the dried and wrinkled flesh tones of the elders and the virtuosic depiction of the sleeve of the man at the left.

Christ disputing with the Doctors was a favourite theme of Caravaggio's followers and Stom's treatment of it reflects several important prototypes. Around 1615, Bartolommeo Manfredi (1582–after 1622), one of the most original Italian Caravaggesques, painted a celebrated canvas of this subject (Uffizi, Florence; Nicolson, 1989, no. 303). Like the present picture, this depicts the figures three-quarter length, with Christ in the centre of the group. The Utrecht Caravaggist, Dirck van Baburen (c.1590–1624) also executed at least four versions of this theme (cf. Nicolson, 1989, nos. 1054 – 5), including one of 1622 (Nasjonalgalleriet, Oslo) which contains a pondering figure at the left that is closely comparable to the man who occupies this position in Stom's picture. This provides proof (if it were needed) that Stom was receptive to the innovations of the Caravaggisti long before he set foot in Italy. Stom himself produced two other, full-length versions of this theme which also show certain affinities with Baburen's painting.[2]

1 All three pictures are first recorded in the collection of Prince Caracciolo, Naples, and passed by marriage in the eighteenth century to Prince Carafa, Naples. Although their provenance is identical, and their subjects obviously interrelated, these three paintings may not have been intended as true pendants. While the two canvases by Stom are the same size (c. 136 x 181 cm), *Tobias healing his father's blindness* is somewhat smaller (123 x 153.5 cm). The most obvious explanation for this is that it has been cut down, a possibility that warrants further investigation. Yet another reason may be the *ad hoc* nature of the cycle itself, which consists of two equally sized works by one artist and a smaller canvas by another. It is conceivable that the original commission was for two paintings by Stom and that, at a later date – when the latter was no longer available – the patron decided to add a third work to the series. In an attempt to fit it into the cycle, the composition of the *Tobias* was closely modelled on that of *Isaac blessing Jacob*. Though this would still not account for the discrepancies in size, it is worth noting that the three 'philosophers' ordered by Antonio Ruffo from Rembrandt in the 1650s and 1660s were all of a different size and format. The status of *Tobias healing his father's blindness* is further confused by the fact that a variant of this composition attributed to Stom also exists. It was last recorded in the Rospigliosi sale, Tavazzi, Rome, 12–24 December 1932 (375) and measured 156 x 213 cm. (Photo: Witt Library)

Christ disputing with the Doctors was sold Sotheby's, 5 July 1989, lot 7; and *Tobias healing his father's blindness* was sold Sotheby's, Parke-Bernet, New York, 1 June 1990, lot 71. The latter was exhibited in *Battistello Caracciolo e il primo naturalismo a Napoli*, Castel Sant 'Elmo, Naples, 1991, p. 311, no. 2.74.

2 Cf. *Holländische Malerei in neuem Licht, Hendrick ter Brugghen und seine Zeitgenossen*, Centraal Museum, Utrecht and Herzog Anton Ulrich-Museum, Braunschweig, 1986-7, pp. 337 – 42, nos. 76 – 7 (for all three of Stom's paintings of *Christ disputing with the Doctors*).

3 A Man with a Glass of Wine, Pipe and Fiddle,
c. 1625
[Fig. 4, p. 16]

Oil on canvas, 86 x 66 cm.

Kingston Lacy, The Bankes Collection
(The National Trust)

The subject of a half-length musician was a favourite one with the Utrecht Caravaggisti and appears to have originated with Terbrugghen, whose pendant paintings of Flute Players (Gemäldegalerie, Kassel) of 1621 are unquestionably the finest of all works on this theme. In the same year, Terbrugghen's former master, Abraham Bloemaert, painted another *Flute Player* (Centraal Museum, Utrecht), dramatically lit by candlelight – a clear indication of his sudden infatuation with the Caravaggesque style.

This painting was probably executed soon after and was regarded by Nicolson (1977, p. 240) as Stom's earliest surviving work. Weaknesses in the draughtsmanship lend support to this view, among them the unnaturally short neck of the violin, the large size of the man's hands, and the misalignment of his mouth, which does not recede correctly. The handling of paint, however, appears unusually audacious, especially in the agitated highlights of the sleeve and in the plume in the man's hat, where the artist has scored into the paint with the butt end of the brush to reveal the light ochre underpainting.

The picture's subject would appear to be straightforward, though it is worth noting that both drinking and smoking

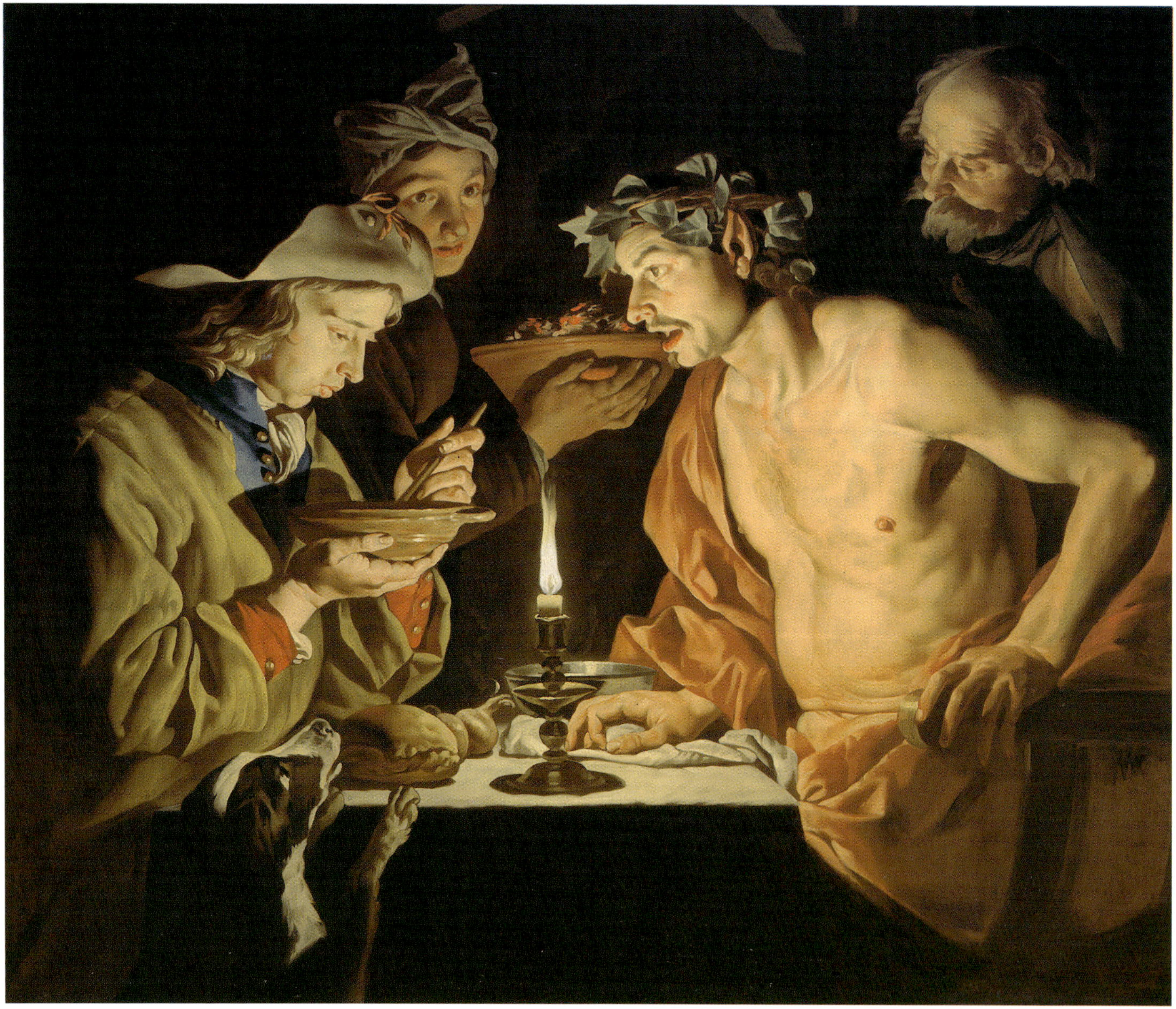

Fig. 18 (No. 4), Matthias Stom, *Satyr with Peasant Family*,
Collection of Brian Sewell

were frowned upon by moralists in the seventeenth century and that the violin often had sexual connotations associated with virility.

Though Stom executed numerous other half-length genre paintings throughout his career (cf. fig. 22), few of these depict musicians. Instead, he favoured figures lighting or holding a candle or firebrand.

The present picture is first recorded in the collection of Sir Ralph Bankes at Gray's Inn, London, in 1656/8 and was attributed to Hals, Gerard Seghers and Honthorst before being given to Stom.[1] It has been specially cleaned for this exhibition.

1 Typescript of a forthcoming catalogue entry on the picture (dated 20 April 1999) by Alistair Laing, who lists the painting as 'attributed to Matthias Stom' and notes that it is 'an untypical work for him'. While such doubts are understandable, the painting is here retained as an autograph work on the grounds of its apparent immaturity – a hypothesis that will only be tested when it is confronted with other pictures by Stom in the exhibition. I am grateful to Alistair Laing for making his text available to me.

4 **Satyr with Peasant Family**

('Blowing hot and blowing cold'), c.1628
[Fig. 18]

Oil on canvas, 118.1 x 136 cm.

Collection of Brian Sewell

The subject of this picture was popular with Dutch and Flemish artists of the seventeenth century and originates in Aesop's *Fables*:

It is said that once a man entered into a friendship with a satyr. Winter had come and the cold weather with it, so the man raised his hands to his mouth and blew upon them. The satyr asked him why he did that. The man replied that he was warming his hands because of the cold.

Then they were served a meal. As the food was very hot, the man took it in small portions, raised them to his mouth, and blew on them. The satyr again asked him why he acted thus. The man replied that it cooled his meal because it was hot.

'Oh well, friend,' said the satyr, 'I give up on your friendship, because you blow hot and cold with the same mouth.'

Stom painted two canvases of this theme, one with five figures (Nicolson, 1989, no. 1488) and the present picture, with four. In both of these, the figure blowing upon his bowl is a young boy, whose action meets with consternation and surprise by the satyr. These two figures are shown seated at a table lit by a candle and accompanied by two servants. At the lower left, a leaping dog reacts to the appearance of the meal in a pose similar to its counterpart in *Isaac blessing Jacob* (fig. 1). The relationship between the youth with the bowl and the maidservant behind him is also closely comparable to that in the Barber Institute's picture and exemplifies Stom's habit of repeating certain compositional ideas, even when treating very different themes.

The picture would appear to be among Stom's earliest Caravaggesque canvases and may well date from before he settled in Italy. There are several reasons for supposing this, the most obvious of which is the theme. With its combination of peasant genre and classical erudition, the subject was much favoured by Northern artists but rarely depicted in Italy. Popularised by the Dutch poet Joost van den Vondel, the theme was repeatedly painted by Jacob Jordaens in a boisterous and raucous manner that is the antithesis of the elegance of Stom. The style of the present picture also seems close to that of Stom's pre-Caravaggesque works in its delicate palette of silvery blue, pale olive and peach pink and in its smooth and idealised facial types. Though Nicolson (1977, p. 241) dated both of Stom's versions of this theme to his early years in Naples, they may be among the Caravaggesque canvases executed in the (?) decade or so after he reached maturity, when he was still residing in the North.

5 Salome receiving the Head of John the Baptist, c.1628–30
[Fig. 12, p. 32]

Oil on canvas, 109.2 x 155.7 cm.

Collection of Sir Denis Mahon

The subject of this picture is from Mark VI, 16 – 29. When John the Baptist rebuked Herod for marrying Herodias, the wife of his brother, he was imprisoned. Herod then held a banquet at which his stepdaughter Salome danced before him. Transported by this, Herod decided to grant Salome any wish, whereupon Herodias instructed her to demand the head of the Baptist. The King then sent an executioner to behead him in prison and the head was delivered to Salome, who presented it to Herodias.

Stom depicts the executioner delivering the head to a plate held out by Salome, who appears transfixed by it. To her right, Herodias looks on in triumph at the success of her plan. In the foreground, a youth holds a candle which illuminates the group, its flickering light intensifying the dramatic action.

The picture is widely regarded as among the artist's earliest Caravaggesque works. The existence of a copy of it by William Dobson (fig. 13), which was made in London c. 1640, suggests that the original may have been executed in northern Europe, before Stom's journey to Italy, and imported into England shortly thereafter. The style of the work supports this, especially in the highly idealised profile of Salome, which closely resembles comparable figures by Rubens of the mid 1610s.[1] Also suggesting an early date is the somewhat awkward position of the head of the Baptist, which is not in the same plane as the executioner's arm. A final indication of the picture's comparative 'immaturity' is its relatively undramatic treatment of the theme. This is especially apparent in the benevolent expressions of the executioner and Salome, both of whom appear too kindly to have committed such a gruesome deed.

Stom apparently never painted this subject again, though he did execute two full-length versions of the *Beheading of John the Baptist* (Nicolson, 1989, nos. 1470 and 1551).

The present picture has been specially cleaned for this exhibition and is here shown with the copy by Dobson for the first time since the latter was completed.

1 Nicolson (1977, p. 240) draws a comparison with van Dyck's *Continence of Scipio* (Christ Church, Oxford) of 1620–21, but the figure may also be compared with the head of Agrippina in Rubens's *Tiberius and Agrippina* (National Gallery of Art, Washington) of c.1614.

Reference: *Discovering the Italian Baroque, The Denis Mahon Collection*, by Gabriele Finaldi and Michael Kitson, The National Gallery, London, 1997, pp. 162-3, no. 77.

6 The Adoration of the Shepherds, c.1635
[Fig. 19]

Oil on canvas, 124.5 x 175.5 cm.

Leeds Museums and Galleries
(Temple Newsam House)

More than a dozen paintings of the Adoration of the Shepherds survive by Stom, making it the most frequently depicted theme in his art. These range from large, full-length versions featuring more than ten figures to more intimate, half-length compositions containing only five or six. This picture is characteristic of the latter group and consists of three shepherds worshipping the Christ Child, who is presented by the Virgin. Behind her Joseph appears, emerging from the shadows. In virtually all of these works, the Holy Family is shown at the left or right of the composition and the shepherds on the opposite side, a scheme which derives from Honthorst's *Adoration*

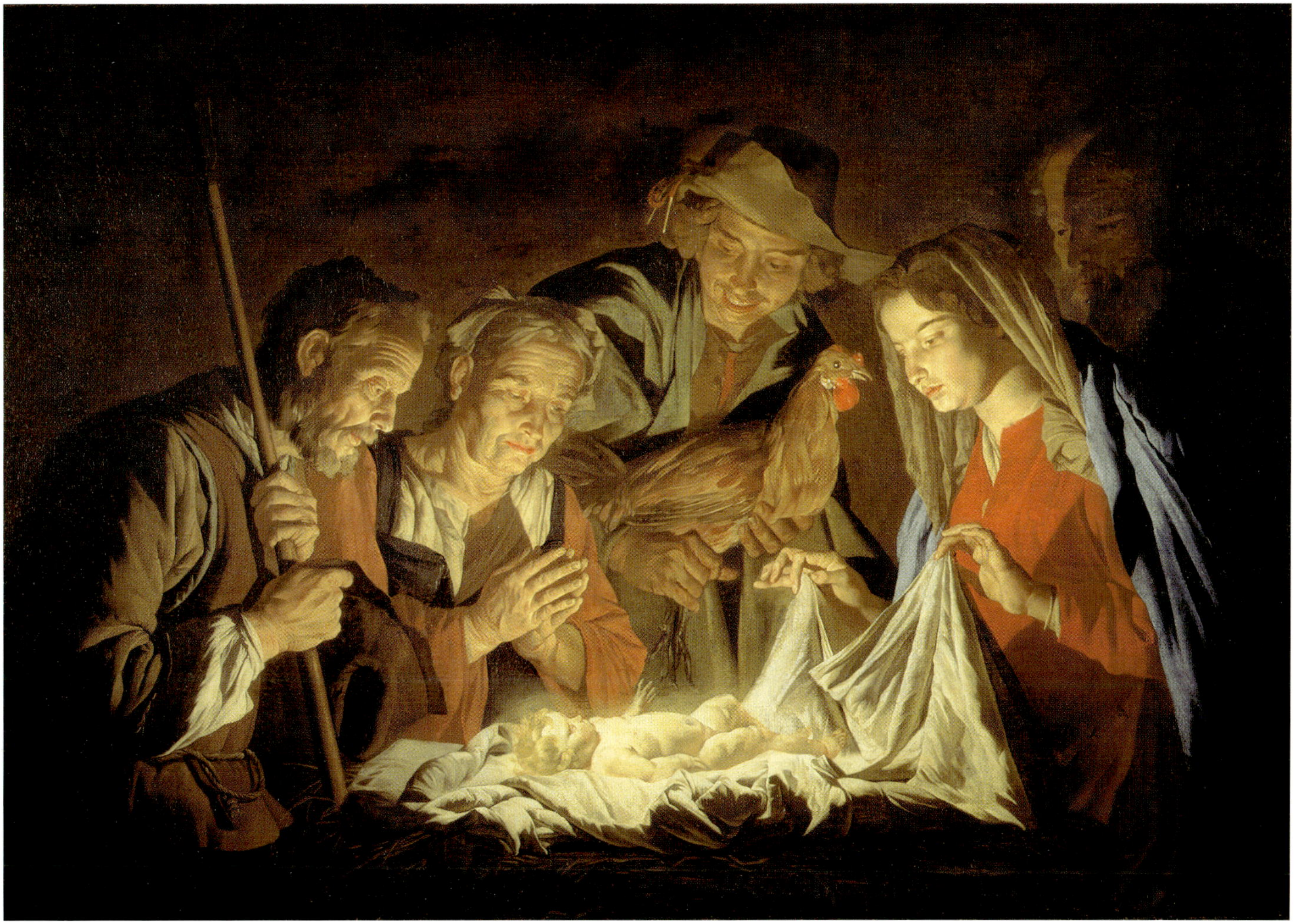

Fig. 19 (No. 6), Matthias Stom, *The Adoration of the Shepherds*,
Leeds Museums and Galleries (Temple Newsam House)

of the Shepherds of 1617 and *Nativity with two Angels* (both Uffizi, Florence; the latter destroyed 1993) of 1620, which Stom must have known.

This painting repeats, in reverse, the design of a similar work in the Liechtenstein Collection, Vaduz (Nicolson, 1989, no. 1513), which depicts an aged couple kneeling devoutly before the Christ Child while a younger shepherd stands, bearing a gift for the Saviour. In the Vaduz picture, this is a basket containing the carcass of a duck, whereas here it is a live cock. Though the latter often serves as a symbol of the Passion, through its association with the Denial of St Peter, it is unlikely to mean this here. More probably it indicates the rustic simplicity of the shepherds. The cock also lends an engagingly domestic touch to the painting, which is one of humble people rapt in adoration at the sudden sight of a miracle – that of the infant Saviour. From him radiates the light that illuminates the group, seemingly quivering over the furrowed brows of the aged shepherds. But the deeper significance of this miracle is not lost on Stom. For, as the Virgin lifts the drapery to reveal the Christ Child, he appears isolated and vulnerable.

The present painting has been specially cleaned for this exhibition.

7 **Christ before Pilate**, c.1635
[Fig. 20]

Oil on canvas, 152.4 x 203.2 cm.

Private Collection, United Kingdom

This is one of three surviving canvases by Stom modelled on Honthorst's *Christ before the High Priest* (fig. 21) of c.1618 in the National Gallery, London, which was in the Giustiniani Collection in Rome until 1804. Two of these depict Christ before the High Priest (Ackland Art Museum, The University of North Carolina, Chapel Hill and Private Collection, Sweden). The present picture appears instead to portray Christ before Pilate, who is shown very similarly dressed in Stom's *Pilate washing his Hands* in the Louvre.[1]

With his wrists bound, Christ has been brought before Pilate by the Jews, who threaten violence and demand that he be crucified. His hands pressed to his chest, Pilate appears to be interrogating the prisoner: 'Art thou the King of the Jews?' This episode is recounted in all four Gospels (Matthew XXVII, 11 – 26; Mark XV, 2 – 15; Luke XXIII, 13 – 25; John XVIII, 28 – 40). Though they indicate that the confrontation took place by daylight, Stom portrays it as a night scene, illuminated by torchlight.

The picture is an outstanding example of Stom's unabashedly theatrical style and hinges upon a clenched fist brandished by one of the Jews, in the exact centre of the composition. At the right Pilate sits enthroned, his tense and furrowed draperies and gnarled profile vividly conveying his ensnaring role in the action. On the opposite side, Christ is surrounded by four of his Jewish tormentors, one of whom lurks in the shadows of the background to the immediate left of him. His head bowed in abject resignation, Christ is confronted by a sword-bearing youth in armour who wears a louche and seemingly crazed expression as he raises his threatening fist. This explosive gesture is greeted with leering satisfaction by a rubicund figure, worthy of Frans Hals, who gazes directly out at the viewer. At the far left, another tormentor clasps Christ's arm and shoulder. Dramatically profiled, he opens his mouth in a jeering expression, as though demanding the prisoner's execution.

The present picture was sold at Christie's on 18 December 1936 (lot 77) with an attribution to Honthorst. A drawing after it, in the British Museum,[2] is one of 277 drawings commissioned by Cecil Brownlow, 9th Earl of Exeter from the German artist Nikolas Mosmann (c.1727–87) after notable works of art to be seen in Italy.

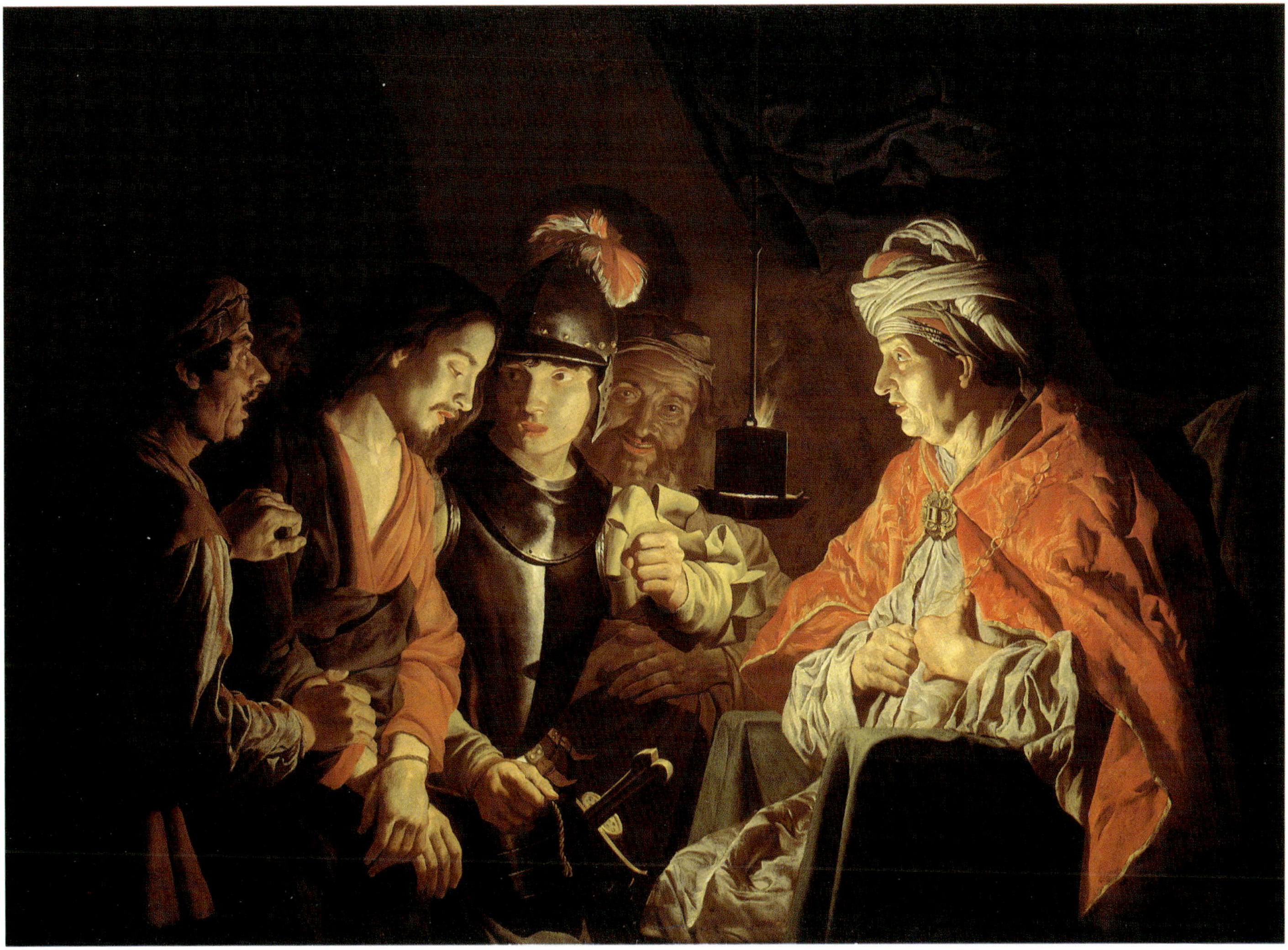

Fig. 20 (No. 7), Matthias Stom, *Christ before Pilate*,
Private Collection, United Kingdom

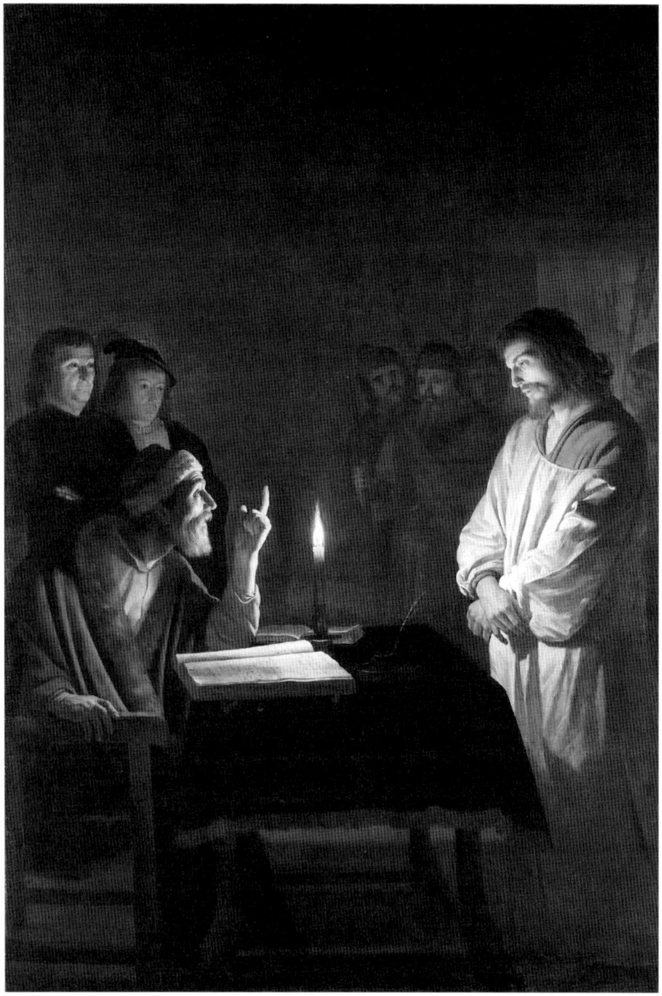

Fig. 21, Gerrit van Honthorst, *Christ before the High Priest*, The National Gallery, London

Mosmann was in Rome between 1757 and his death in 1787 and noted on his copy of *Christ before Pilate* – which he inevitably attributed to Honthorst – that the picture was in the possession of the dealer, Thomas Jenkins, in Rome. There it formed one of a series of twelve identically sized canvases 'by' Honthorst which depicted episodes from the Passion of Christ. Circumstantial evidence suggests that these were identical to a cycle of paintings by Stom recorded in the Capuchin Church of S. Efremo Nuovo, Naples, in 1692, and subsequently dispersed. This cycle – which may well have consisted of more than the twelve canvases owned by Jenkins – must have been the crowning achievement of Stom's Neapolitan years.[3]

1 Cf. *Le Siècle de Rembrandt, Tableaux hollandais des collections publiques françaises*, Musée du Petit Palais, Paris, 1970, p. 212, no. 205.

2 German, Mosmann, Portfolio 6, Basement XIIIC, T. 4.–47.

3 The complicated history of this cycle is fully and convincingly recounted in an undated typescript in my possession (received 20 July 1998) by Henry Avar. I am very grateful to Mr Avar for making this available to me.

8 **Old Woman and Boy by Candlelight**, c.1635 [Fig. 22]

Oil on canvas, 58.4 x 71.1 cm.

Birmingham Museums and Art Gallery

This is one of more than two dozen paintings by Stom depicting half-length figures lit by a candle or firebrand. Though there is no reason to suppose that it is intended as an allegory, the theme itself has a venerable history. Pliny the Elder (*Historia Naturalis* XXXV, 138) notes that the ancient painter Antiphilos was praised for his portrayal of 'a boy blowing a fire', because of the reflections thrown on the boy's face. This theme re-emerged in the sixteenth century, when it acquired numerous connotations, with the action of blowing on flame associated with the passion of lust and the candle itself with the theme of transience. If Stom intended any deeper meaning in the present work, it is likely to be the latter. The picture portrays an old woman holding a candle while a young boy looks longingly on, as though waiting for her to pass the flame to him. Their relationship reminds one of the ancient adage that 'generations of living things pass in swift

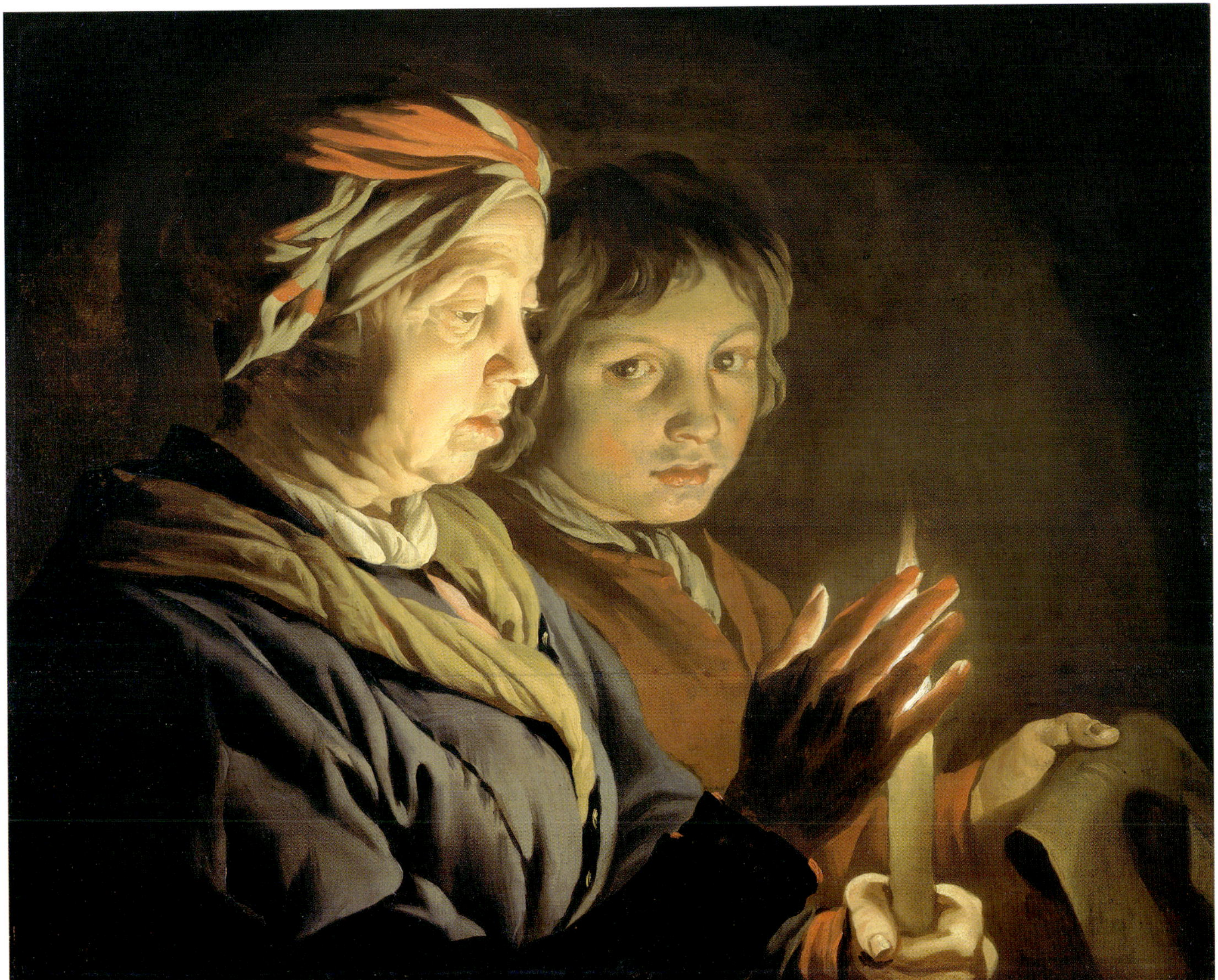

Fig. 22 (No. 8), Matthias Stom, *Old Woman and Boy by Candlelight*,
Birmingham Museums and Art Gallery

succession and like runners hand on the torch of life' (Lucretius, *De Rerum Natura*, II, 79) – a popular maxim that was revived in the Renaissance.

The picture is remarkable for its sensitive exploration of the play of light over both figures and for its broad and buttery application of paint, which testifies to the fluency of Stom's technique, even when working on a small scale. Though it is impossible to date the work, its freedom and skill suggest that it is a product of the artist's full maturity and contrast strikingly with the gaucheries of the *Man with a Glass of Wine, Pipe and Fiddle* (fig. 4).

9 The Evangelists Mark and Luke, c.1635 [Fig. 23]

Oil on canvas, 113 x 154 cm.

Trafalgar Galleries, London

Stom was evidently familiar with the two traditional ways of depicting the Four Evangelists in the sixteenth and seventeenth centuries: either (1) in four separate half-length canvases or (2) grouped together in a single picture and writing or reading their gospels around a table. The first type was much favoured by such Utrecht painters as Wtewael, Bloemaert and Terbrugghen and also portrayed by Stom himself, whose *St John* and *St Mark* (Musée des Beaux-Arts, Rennes; Nicolson, 1989, nos. 1466 – 7) originally formed part of such a series.

The present picture belongs to neither category and portrays Mark and Luke seated with their attributes, the lion and ox, and holding a large book. They are depicted full-length, the dramatically foreshortened Luke with his head downcast, writing his gospel. To the left, Mark gazes directly out at the viewer, his left hand holding up a volume inscribed *Pax tibi, Marce, evangelista meus*. This refers to the words Christ spoke to him when he visited him in prison and may be translated as: 'Peace be with you, Mark, my evangelist.'

A pendant picture, depicting the evangelists Matthew and John (fig. 24) shows these figures facing in the opposite direction and was clearly designed to hang to the right of the present painting. In their earthy palette, dramatic lighting and intensely realistic figures, both works testify to Stom's absorption in the art of Caravaggio, especially the first version of his *St Matthew and the Angel* (formerly Berlin; destroyed), painted for the Contarelli Chapel, S. Luigi dei Francesi in 1602 and rejected by the church authorities on the grounds of decorum. The figure of St Luke in this picture – with his bald pate, weathered features and prominent, bare feet – seems directly modelled on Caravaggio's equally plebeian

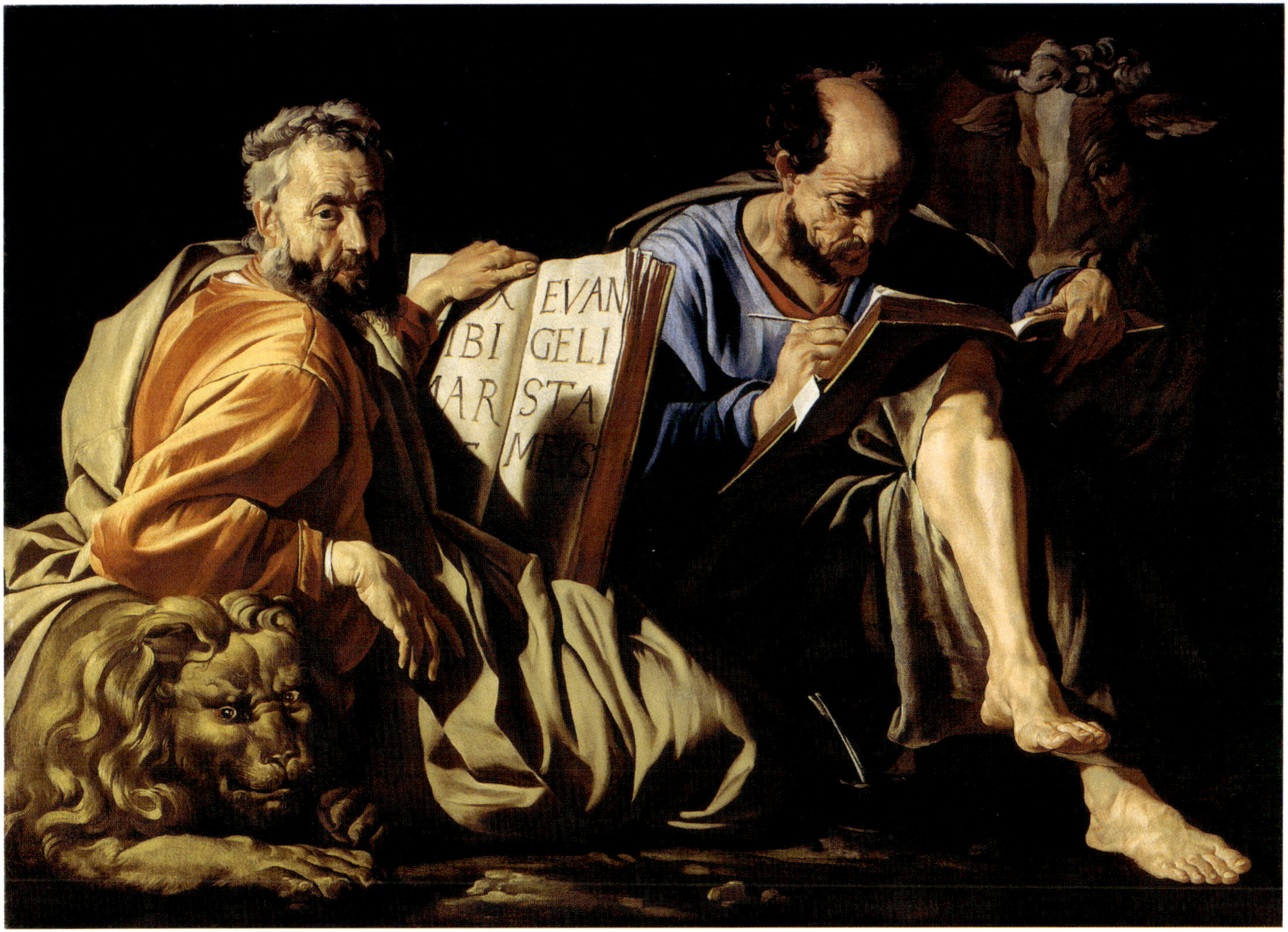

Fig 23 (No. 9), Matthias Stom, *The Evangelists Mark and Luke*,
Trafalgar Galleries, London

figure and is among Stom's most obvious debts to his great predecessor. Adding to the vigour and earthiness of the picture are the clay-like fleshtones and coppery blues and oranges of the evangelists' mantles.

Stom introduced a further subtlety in his paintings of the Four Evangelists. While the figures in this picture are shown

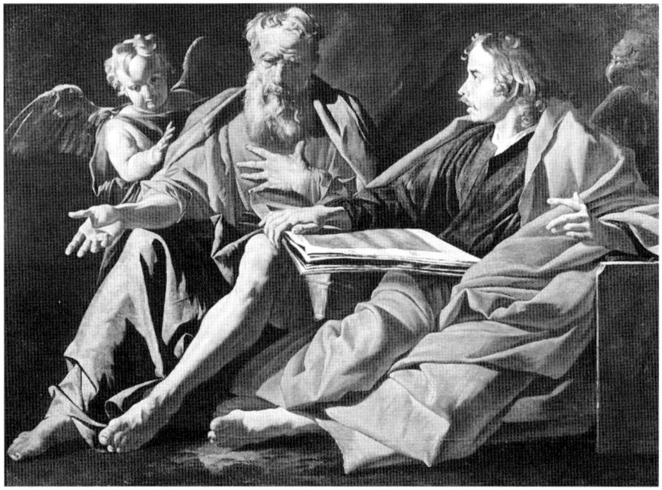

Fig. 24, Matthias Stom, *The Evangelists Matthew and John*, Columbia University, New York

in self-absorbed poses, meditating or writing, the pendant portrays Matthew and John engaged in an animated discourse, as though discussing their separate accounts of the gospels. Their poses derive not from traditional treatments of the Four Evangelists but from the related theme of the Four Fathers of the Church, conversing and gesticulating over the miracle of the Holy Sacrament.[1] This is reflected in two comparable works by Stom depicting *St Augustine* and *St Gregory the Great* (Kunstmuseum, Basel; Nicolson, 1989, nos. 1468 – 9), which must originally have formed part of a set of four canvases of the church fathers.

1 Cf. John Walsh Jr., 'Stomer's Evangelists', *The Burlington Magazine*, CXVIII, July 1976, pp. 504, 507–8.

Reference: *Trafalgar Galleries at the Royal Academy II,* London, 1979, pp. 50–3, no. 21.

Related Works

10 Govaert Flinck (1615–60)

Isaac blessing Jacob, 1638
[Fig. 10, p. 28]

Oil on canvas, 117 x 141 cm.

Formerly signed upper right: *G Flinck 1638*

Rijksmuseum, Amsterdam

Of the many paintings of *Isaac blessing Jacob* by Rembrandt's pupils, this is probably the most celebrated. It is also the one closest in conception to Stom's version of the theme, prompting one to wonder if both works derive from a common source.

The picture depicts the climactic moment of the story. Touching Jacob's right hand, and convinced that it is that of his hairy brother, Esau, Isaac raises his hand in blessing. Behind him Rebecca gazes warily at her husband, her lips parted, as though urging him on. At the background left is the meal prepared for Isaac. Another version of the same subject by Flinck (Netherlands Institute for Cultural Heritage, Rijswijk, Amsterdam, on loan to the Museum Catharijnconvent, Utrecht), which dates from c.1637, depicts the identical moment, though the figure group is less compact and the mood less conspiratorial.

Flinck studied with Rembrandt in 1633–4 and was one of his most gifted pupils. This is apparent in the sensitive delineation of emotion in this picture. Isaac is depicted as a frail and faltering old man; Rebecca as a wily accomplice, eagerly anticipating the success of her plan; and Jacob appears at once fearful and anxious to ingratiate himself with his blind father. Adding to the warmth and humanity of the scene are the rich, glowing colours and the caressing contours of the bedding and overhanging drape. The inspiration for both of these was probably Rembrandt's *Danae* (Hermitage, St Petersburg), which was begun in c.1636 and must have been known to Flinck. The old crone in Rembrandt's canvas may also have provided Flinck with the model for the Rebecca depicted here.

Though Rembrandt never painted the subject of Isaac blessing Jacob, the large number of versions of it executed by his pupils has led several critics to suggest that the master set the theme as an exercise in the depiction of emotion. Another subject that also exists in large numbers, but was never painted by the master himself, is the Dismissal of Hagar (Genesis XXI, 9–14). Interestingly, both subjects are not only deeply expressive but also involve contending emotions – one of the favourite concerns of Rembrandt's own art. Flinck's success in treating these is especially apparent in the combination of diffidence and desire of Jacob in the present picture.

The painting has recently been restored and cleaned in the Rijksmuseum. Though it was recorded as signed and dated in the late-nineteenth century, this inscription is no longer visible. A highly finished compositional drawing for it, executed in chalk and wash, is in the Museum Boymans-van Beuningen, Rotterdam.[1]

1 Jeroen Giltaij, *The drawings by Rembrandt and his school in the Museum Boymans-van Beuningen*, Rotterdam, 1988, pp. 160–1, no. 71.

Reference: J. W. von Moltke, *Govaert Flinck 1615–1660*, Amsterdam, 1965, p. 17 and pp. 66–7, no. 8.

11 Luca Giordano (1632–1705)

Isaac blessing Jacob, c.1650–3
[Fig. 11, p. 30]

Oil on canvas, 140 x 186 cm.

Signed lower left: *Jordanus F.*

Count Harrach Family Collection, Schloss Rohrau, Lower Austria

This impressive canvas is among the earliest surviving works by Giordano, who became the leading figure in Neapolitan painting in the second half of the seventeenth century. A deeply impressionable artist, Giordano modelled his early works on the paintings by his predecessors to be seen in Naples, especially those of the Spanish master Jusepe de Ribera (1591 – 1652), whose death coincided with the start of his own career. This is apparent in the present picture, which treats the same theme as the celebrated canvas by Ribera of 1637 (fig. 9). Also indebted to the latter are the plebeian figure types, the guise of Jacob – whose arms are covered in goatskin – and the broad and textured application of paint.

Other features of the picture derive instead from Stom's *Isaac blessing Jacob* (fig. 1), which was also in a Neapolitan collection during these years. Among these are the pose of Isaac, the arrangement of the pillow and bedding and the stark black background, with its overhanging drape. The format and dimensions of the canvas are also virtually identical to those of Stom's picture and prompt one to wonder whether Giordano's painting was undertaken in conscious emulation of the former.

When compared with Stom's canvas, however, Giordano's treatment appears much less emotionally charged and fails to explore the psychological undercurrents that are implicit in the theme. As Jacob bows down to touch his father, the latter delivers the blessing in a relaxed and inauspicious manner that lacks the tension and strain of Stom's comparable gesture. Cowering behind Jacob is Rebecca, who merely nudges him forward rather than assuming the more devious and intrusive role of her counterpart in Stom's picture.

The style of the works also differs considerably and reveals the generational divide between the two artists. Stom's painting is executed with the boldly contrasting colours, sharply focused figures and theatrical lighting typical of early Caravaggesque painting – features that imbue his work with an electrifying charge that seems genuinely revelatory. Giordano employs instead the sombre palette, painterly technique and diffused lighting of Ribera and his followers, which may be seen as a kind of diluted Caravaggism that aims to emphasise the earthy realism of the scene.

Though the provenance of this picture is unknown, Ferdinand Bonaventura, Count of Harrach – who established the family's collection – is documented as visiting Giordano in his studio in the Buen Retiro Palace, Madrid on 1 October 1697, when the artist was working for the King of Spain, Charles II. There the Count is recorded as having admired the artist's early works (including the present picture?) far more than his recent paintings.[1]

1 *Galerie Harrach in Wien*, Vienna, 1926, p. iv.

Reference: Oreste Ferrari and Giuseppe Scavizzi, *Luca Giordano, L'opera completa*, Naples, 1992, Vol. I, pp. 31 and 253, no. A20.

12 William Dobson (1611–46), after Stom

Salome receiving the Head of John the Baptist, c.1640 [Fig. 13, p. 33]

Oil on canvas, 110.5 x 130.2 cm.

Board of Trustees of the National Museums and Galleries on Merseyside (Walker Art Gallery, Liverpool)

The only English Caravaggesque picture to survive, this is a copy of a painting by Stom (fig. 12). It reproduces the original faithfully, though Dobson gives Salome more animated and individualised facial features and different jewellery. The torch held by the youth also appears less stylised in the copy and the handling of paint more broken and agitated. The absence of the executioner's right arm makes it likely that the copy has been cut by about 25 cm at the left. Originally the two works were apparently the same size.

The picture is first recorded in 1731, in the collection of the Earl of Pembroke, by Gambarini, who noted that it was Dobson's most important history painting and that, as long as the artist lived, he refused to part with it.[1] It passed as Dobson's own invention until 1952, when Stom's canvas came to light, though as early as 1854, Waagen observed that it appeared indebted to Honthorst.[2] Its fame is further evident in a copy made after it by Isaac Fuller (?1606–72), which is now lost, and in a mezzotint by John Dean (fig. 32).

William Dobson was the most accomplished native-born English painter of the seventeenth century. He is first recorded in 1642 at Oxford, painting the King, his family and his supporters at the wartime court. He left there in 1646 and died in London in the same year. Although his style was much influenced by van Dyck, he painted few subject pictures and none of his surviving works remotely resembles the present picture.

1 C. Gambarini, *Description of the Earl of Pembroke's Pictures*, 1731, p. XI, 79.
2 G. F. Waagen, *Treasures of Art in Great Britain*, London, 1854, III, p. 154.

Reference: *William Dobson 1611–46*, by Malcolm Rogers, National Portrait Gallery, London, 1983, p. 27, no.4.

13 Agostino Veneziano (c. 1490–? after 1536), after Raphael

Isaac blessing Jacob, 1524
[Fig. 6, p. 21]

Engraving, 23.4 x 31.2 cm.

The British Museum

In 1518–19 Raphael and his workshop designed 52 scenes from the Bible for the Loggia of the Vatican. These were painted in fresco in 13 bays, each of which consists of a flattened vault containing four scenes. Twelve of these were devoted to subjects from the Old Testament and one to episodes from the life of Christ. Though experts disagree on the extent of Raphael's direct participation in this scheme, he is usually assumed to have devised all of the compositions, which were then executed largely by members of his workshop, especially Giulio Romano and Giovanni Francesco Penni. The importance of the designs themselves cannot be overestimated. As one of the largest cycles of Old Testament subjects by any sixteenth-century master, they exerted an immense influence on later artists, among them Poussin.

This engraving is based on Raphael's design of *Isaac blessing Jacob*, which is followed in the Loggia by a depiction of *Isaac and Esau*, and remains largely faithful to the original, though it adds a male onlooker behind Isaac's raised knee and a more diversified background at the upper left.

The subject is treated in an heroic and rhetorical manner. Jacob kneels before Isaac and offers his father the meal as Rebecca presents him, clasping her young son in a forceful and authoritative manner. Rising from his bed, Isaac blesses Jacob in a commanding gesture, watched by a man and two children. In the background left, Esau returns from the hunt bearing the carcass of a deer.

The print is inscribed at the upper right acknowledging Raphael as the inventor and initialled and dated 1524 below. Agostino Veneziano (Agostino dei Musi) was a prolific Venetian engraver who went to Rome in 1516, where he executed numerous prints after Raphael, Michelangelo and Giulio Romano.

The design of this work was regarded as canonical well into the seventeenth century, when it was engraved by Giovanni Lanfranco (1582–1647).[1]

1 *The Illustrated Bartsch, Italian Masters of the sixteenth and seventeenth centuries*, ed. Veronika Birke, New York, 1982, Vol. 40, p. 315, no. 12 (347).

Reference: *The Illustrated Bartsch, The Works of Marcantonio Raimondi and of his school*, ed. Konrad Oberhuber, New York, 1978, p. 15, no. 6–1(7).

14 Martin van Heemskerck (1498–1574), after

Isaac blessing Jacob, 1549
[Fig. 25]

Etching, 24.6 x 19.1 cm.

The British Museum

This is one of eight numbered plates in *The Story of Jacob*, executed in 1549 by Dirck Volkertsz Coornhert after designs by Heemskerck, one of the outstanding Netherlandish artists of the sixteenth century. Heemskerck's original drawing for the composition is in Copenhagen.[1]

Seated beside his bed, Isaac is blessing Jacob, who kneels before him praying. At the left, Rebecca 'presents' the youth, bowing before her husband in a ritualistic manner. In a doorway at the upper left, two additional figures are seen. These may be intended to represent Rebecca and Esau, who is either departing or returning from the hunt. Completing the scene are the grooming dog and dozing cat, the warming fire (complete with firetongs) and the still life of the meal. The identity of the classical herm at the upper right is unclear, but it may simply be intended as a general symbol of the pre-Christian world.

Martin van Heemskerck spent his entire career in Haarlem except for the years between 1532 and 1535, when he was in Rome. He painted religious and mythological works and was also an outstanding portraitist. A striking *Self-portrait* of 1553, showing him against a background of the ruins of the Colosseum, is in the Fitzwilliam Museum, Cambridge.

1 Jan Garff, *Tegninger af Maerten van Heemskerck*, Statens Museum for Kunst, Copenhagen, 1971, no. 27.

Reference: *The New Hollstein, Dutch and Flemish Etchings, Engravings and Woodcuts 1450–1700*, Maarten van Heemskerck, Part I, Amsterdam, 1993, p. 35, no. 24.

15 Ercole Setti (?1530–1607)

Isaac blessing Jacob, c.1570
[Fig. 26, p. 56]

Pen and brown ink, 25.1 x 38.6 cm.

Ashmolean Museum, Oxford

One of the most elaborate of all treatments of the theme, this drawing depicts Isaac blessing Jacob at the extreme right, in a grouping evidently inspired by Raphael's famous fresco of the same subject (cf. fig. 6). Aided by Rebecca, Jacob hands his father the meal and

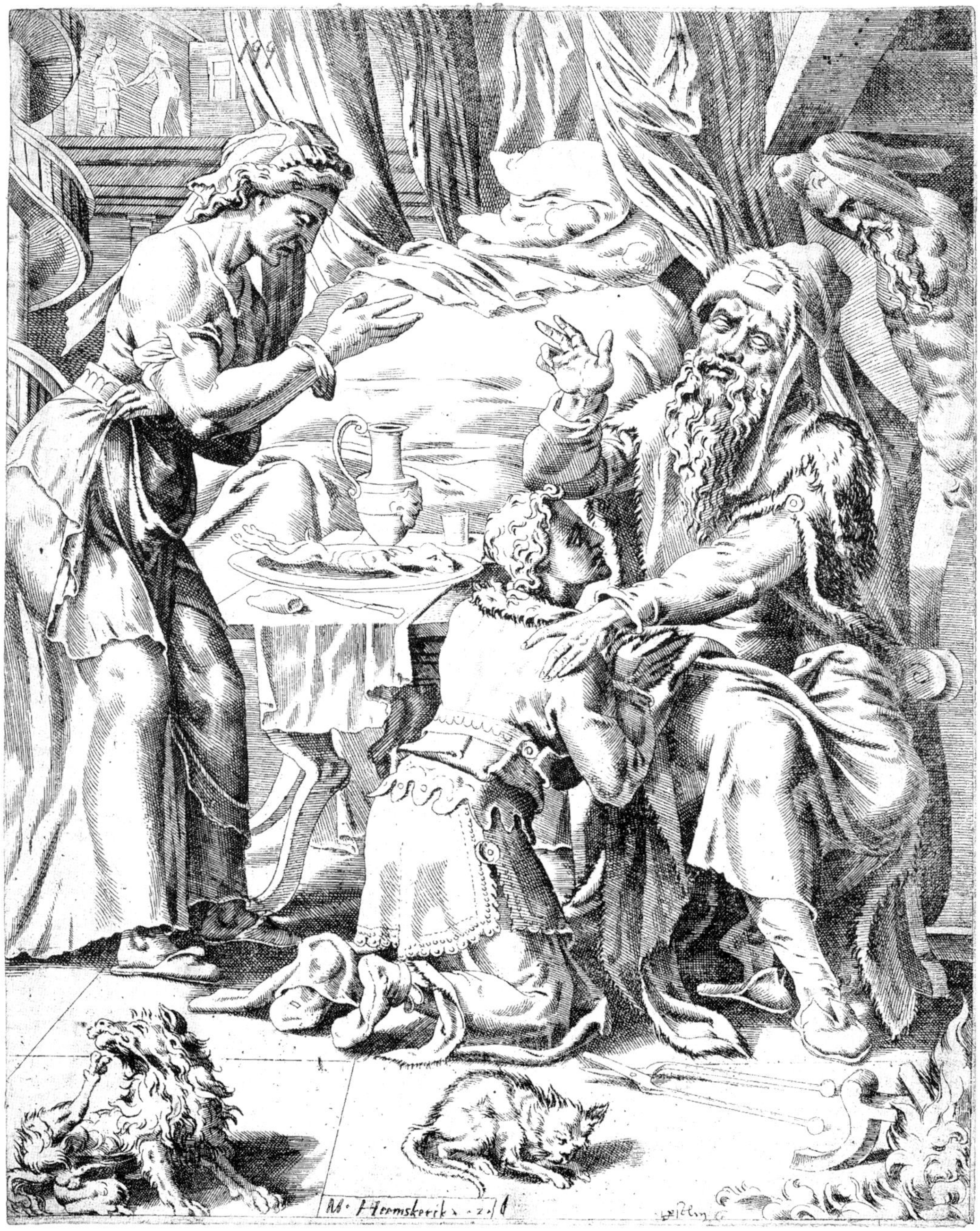

Fig. 25 (No. 14),
Martin van Heemskerck,
Isaac blessing Jacob

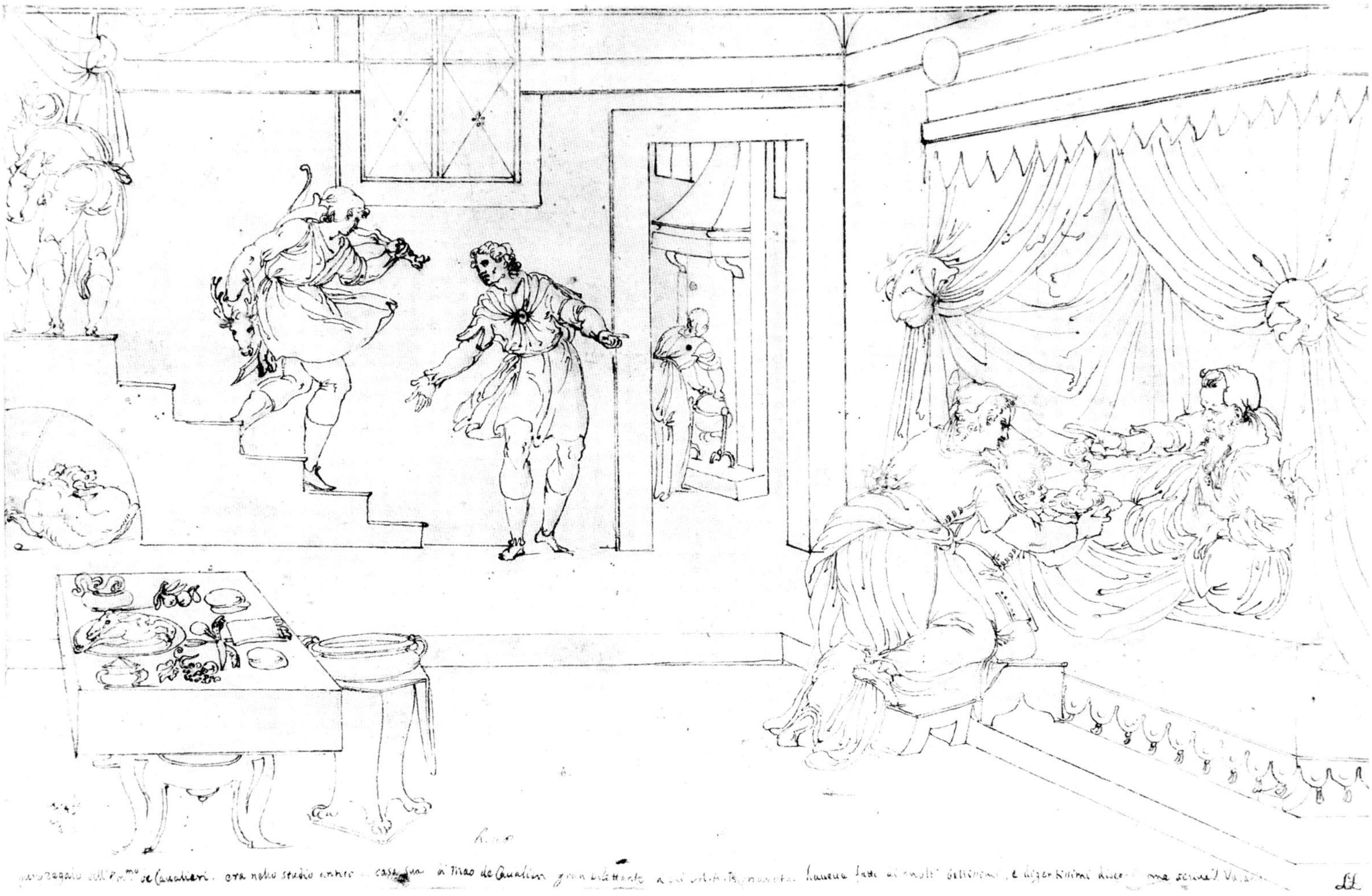

Fig. 26 (No. 15), Ercole Setti, *Isaac blessing Jacob*,
Ashmolean Museum, Oxford

receives the paternal blessing. In the background left, Esau descends a flight of stairs bearing the carcass of a deer. He is greeted by a male servant, while two other figures converse at the top of the stairs. The scene is completed by various domestic motifs, including a female servant working in another room at the background right, a sleeping dog under an arch, and a table laid out with an elaborate meal. The setting is a large interior, the lines of which have been carefully drawn with a ruler.

The drawing is executed entirely in line and is one of only a handful of such works that can be attributed to Setti, a minor mannerist painter who worked in Modena, where he painted a *Marriage Feast at Cana* for the refectory of the Benedictines of S. Pietro, supposedly in 1589. Characteristic of his drawing style are the fluttering skirts and thickly proportioned legs evident here.

The inscription at the bottom is by Padre Resta (1635–1714), who later owned the drawing, and is of great interest. It records that the work was a gift to him from a member of the family of Tommaso de' Cavalieri, a young Roman nobleman to whom Michelangelo became deeply attached in 1532 and who subsequently became the recipient of many of the latter's finest late presentation drawings. Like them, *Isaac blessing Jacob* was almost certainly intended as an independent work of art, rather than as a study for a painting.

References: Walter Vitzthum, 'Drawings by Ercole Setti', *The Burlington Magazine*, XCVII, August 1955, pp. 252 and 254; K.T. Parker, *Catalogue of Drawings in the Ashmolean Museum*, Vol. II, Italian Schools, Oxford, 1956, pp. 375–6, no. 699.

16 Martin de Vos (1532–1603), after

Isaac blessing Jacob, c.1579
[Fig. 7, p. 22]

Engraving, 21.5 x 26.4 cm.

The British Museum

This engraving is part of a History of Jacob and Esau that appeared in an illustrated Bible, the *Thesaurus Veteris et Novi Testamenti* published by Gerard de Jode in Antwerp in 1585. It depicts Isaac blessing Jacob, who kneels before his father in a devout pose, his hands joined in prayer. At the left Rebecca gazes on meditatively; while, in the background right, Esau returns from the hunt accompanied by his dogs. The inscription at the bottom summarises the story and may be translated as follows: 'Jacob is blessed through the persuasion of his mother and is favoured by his father'.

Martin de Vos was one of the leading Flemish masters of the late sixteenth century. He was in Italy in the mid 1550s, where he worked in Rome, Florence and Venice, studying with Tintoretto. A prolific painter of religious works and portraits, he also executed more than 1600 designs for prints. The Michelangelesque pose of Rebecca in this engraving testifies to his study of Italian art.

Reference: *Hollstein's Dutch and Flemish Etchings, Engravings and Woodcuts 1450–1700*, Vol. XLIV, Maarten de Vos, Amsterdam, 1996, p. 21, no. 69.

17 Jan Gillisz van Vliet (1600/10–c. 1668), after Jan Lievens

Isaac and Esau, c.1633–5
[Fig. 27]

Etching, 47 x 38.6 cm.

The British Museum

This etching reproduces a lost painting by Jan Lievens (1607–74), who was a close associate and collaborator of Rembrandt during his early years in Leiden (1625–31). The painting was probably made in c. 1628 and owes a clear debt to Rembrandt, whose *Tobit and Anna* (Rijksmuseum, Amsterdam) of 1626 provided the source for the figures of Isaac and Rebecca in Lievens's composition.

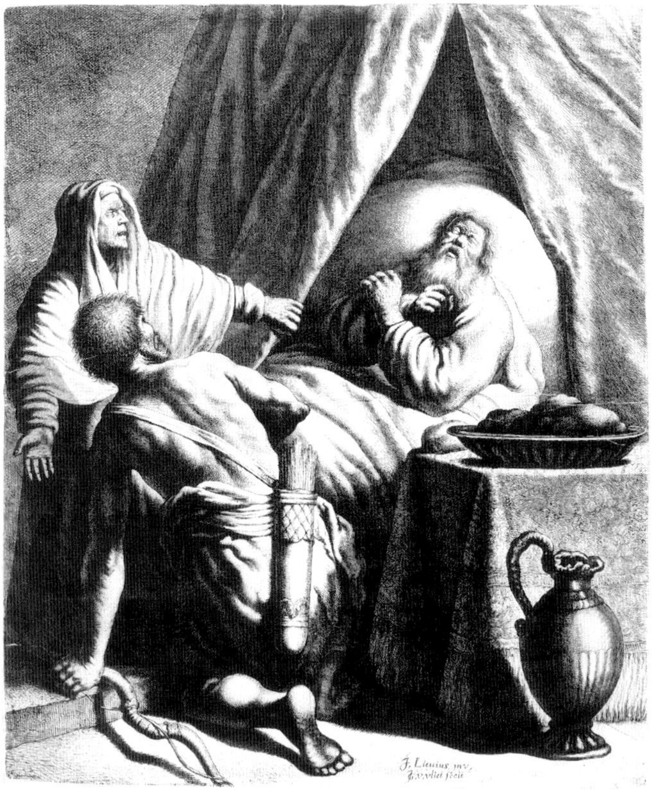

Fig. 27 (No. 17), Jan Gillisz van Vliet (after Lievens), *Isaac and Esau*

The subject is from Genesis XXVII, 30–40 and depicts the conclusion to the story of Isaac blessing Jacob, who has already received the blessing and departed. He is immediately followed by Esau, returned from the hunt with a meal prepared for his father. When Isaac realises that he has been deceived into blessing the wrong son, he trembles with fear but forgoes blessing Esau, noting that he must now serve his brother.

Lievens depicts Esau on his knees, his body recoiling, as though in sudden recognition of his defeat; while the aged Isaac, seated in bed, wrings his hands in terror. At the left, Rebecca shrinks back in horror at the realisation that her secret has been discovered. The full-length presentation of the figures is common in the early works of both Lievens and Rembrandt and derives from their teacher, Peter Lastman (1583–1633).

The large scale and evident skill of this etching made Van Vliet one of the most sought-after reproductive printmakers of his day. During the 1630s he also made a number of ambitious prints after designs by Rembrandt for commercial purposes.

For a drawing of *Isaac and Esau* from the Rembrandt school, see fig. 29.

Reference: *Rembrandt and Van Vliet, A Collaboration on Copper*, Museum het Rembrandthuis, Amsterdam, 1996, pp. 89–90, no. 34.

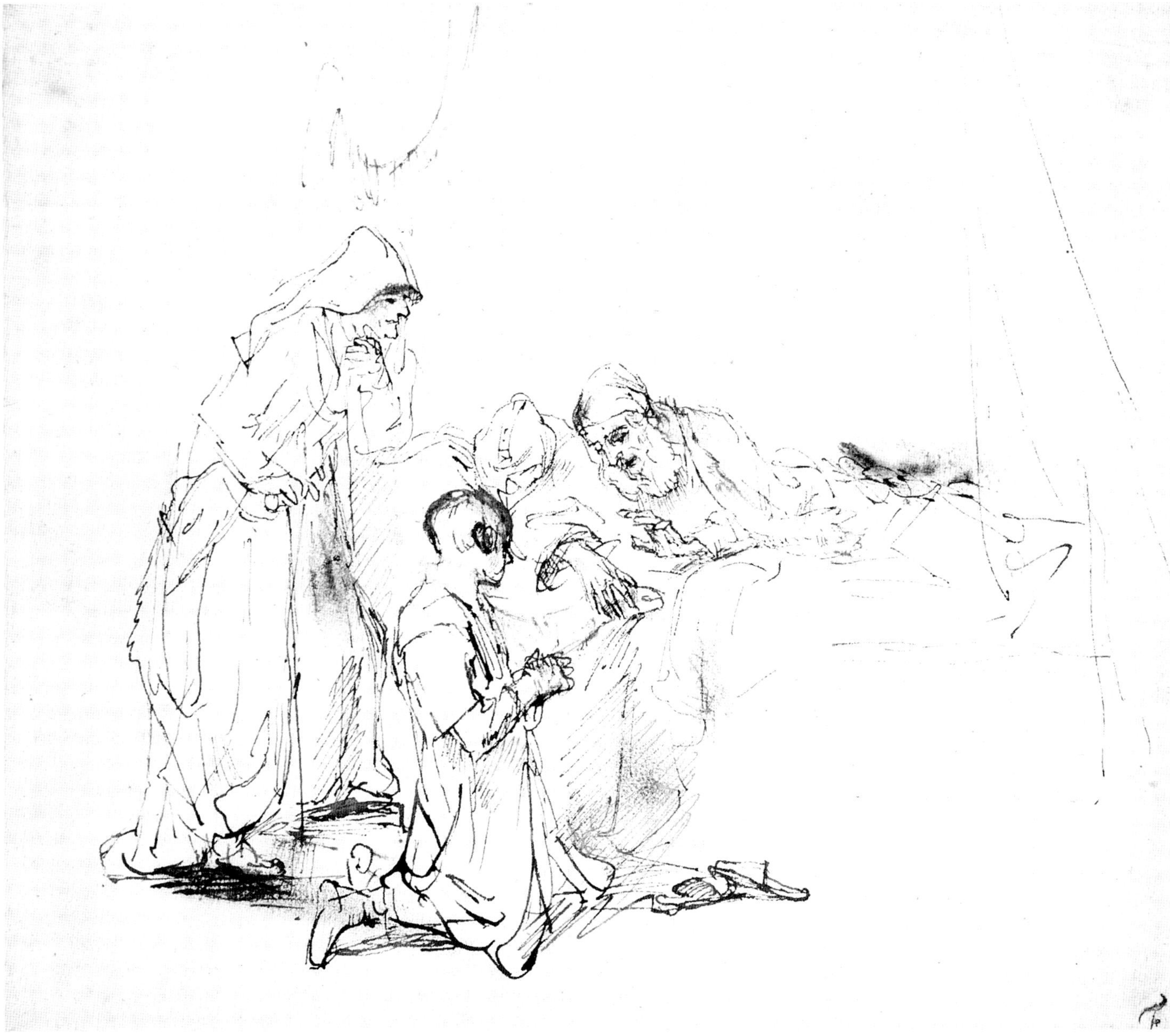

Fig. 28 (No. 18), Rembrandt, *Isaac blessing Jacob*,
The Duke of Devonshire and the Chatsworth Settlement Trustees

18 Rembrandt van Rijn (1606 – 69)

Isaac blessing Jacob, c.1652
[Fig. 28, p. 59]

Pen and brown ink with touches of wash,
17.6 x 19.7 cm.

The Duke of Devonshire and the Chatsworth Settlement Trustees

This is one of only two drawings of *Isaac blessing Jacob* that are unanimously given to Rembrandt, though at least a half dozen others were once attributed to him. With his characteristic humanity, the great Dutch master goes right to the heart of the matter. Absent is the episode of the presentation of the meal, the touching of Jacob's hands, or the connivance of Rebecca. Instead, Rembrandt depicts the blessing itself. Jacob kneels by his father's bedside, his hands clasped in prayer and his head bowed down – a figure of abject humility. Raising himself falteringly from his pillow, Isaac turns and blesses his son in a reverential manner, worthy of a true benediction. Behind them stands Rebecca, her eyes rooted to the spot and her leering mouth silently anticipating the success of the scheme. In her stealthful and wary pose, Rembrandt captures perfectly the deceitful nature of her deed. In contrast to nearly every other artist, Rembrandt avoids portraying any of the protagonists in an emotionally or physically ambivalent state. Isaac is not doubtful, Jacob not fearful, nor Rebecca manipulative. Instead, he presents three figures of benevolence, humility and guile, penetrating to the human essence of the theme.

Rembrandt evidently had an abiding interest in the subject of Isaac blessing Jacob and repeatedly encouraged his pupils to treat it, in both paintings and drawings, probably because of its psychological complexity and striking emotional contrasts. But he never painted the theme itself and rarely even drew it. Instead, when he came to treat a patriarchal blessing from the Old Testament, he chose the subject of Jacob blessing the sons of Joseph (Genesis XLVIII). This is the theme of a magisterial canvas by the artist of 1656 (Gemäldegalerie Alte Meister, Staatliche Museen, Kassel). A much rarer subject, this may have appealed to Rembrandt because it allowed great scope for invention. But there may be another and much more profound reason why he was attracted to it.

In Isaac blessing Jacob, the aged father is deceived as a result of his blindness and infirmity. In Jacob blessing the sons of Joseph, however, the venerable patriarch is gifted with superior knowledge and intuition and chooses to bless Ephraim rather than his brother Manassah, foretelling that the former will be greater than the latter. If the underlying theme of the one subject is the frailty and vulnerability of old age, that of the other is its greater wisdom and spiritual insight – a belief that Rembrandt endorsed in countless other works throughout his career.

On the verso of this drawing is a study of a bearded man in a high cap, facing to the right.

Reference: Otto Benesch, *The Drawings of Rembrandt*, London, 1973, Vol. V, p. 250, no. 891.

19 Imitator of Rembrandt

Isaac and Esau, c.1636
[Fig. 29]

Pen and brown ink with brown wash, 18.5 x 24 cm.

Board of Trustees of the National Museums and Galleries on Merseyside (Walker Art Gallery, Liverpool). Purchased with the aid of contributions from the National Heritage Memorial Fund, the National Art Collections Fund, Sir Denis Mahon and British Nuclear Fuels, 1995.

This drawing depicts the same subject as no. 17. Esau has returned from the hunt and kneels before his father, bearing a quiver and arrows on his back, to demand the paternal blessing. Gesticulating with his left hand, as though in

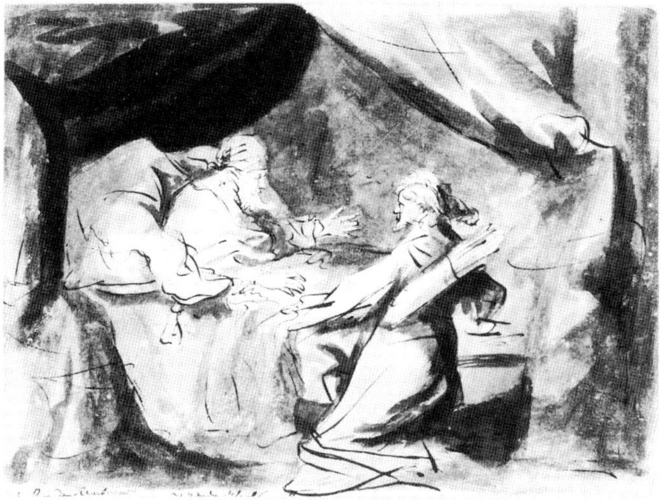

Fig. 29 (No. 19), Imitator of Rembrandt, *Isaac and Esau*, Walker Art Gallery, Liverpool

heated discussion with his son, Isaac refuses this. The lurching pose of Esau vividly conveys his shock and dismay.

The present work is a copy of a drawing by a member of Rembrandt's school that was last traceable in 1951.[1] Whereas the original is executed in pen alone, this drawing contains extensive passages of wash. The style of the original is that of Rembrandt himself in the mid 1630s; and the composition has obvious affinities with that of Flinck's *Isaac blessing Jacob* (fig. 10), which is also datable to these years.

The drawing has an illustrious history. It is first recorded in 1816 in the sale of the collection of the lawyer, banker and historian William Roscoe (1753–1851), whose outstanding collection of early Italian and Flemish paintings now forms the core of the Walker Art Gallery, Liverpool. Its next owner was Charles Blundell (1761–1837), who purchased 161 of Roscoe's drawings at this sale. His collection remained largely intact in the possession of the Weld-Blundell family until it was acquired by the Walker Art Gallery in 1995.

1 Sold Sotheby's, 7 November 1951, lot 24.

Reference: *Mantegna to Rubens, the Weld-Blundell Drawings Collection*, by Xanthe Brooke, Walker Art Gallery, Liverpool, 1998, p. 193.

20 Jacob Jordaens (1593–1678)

Isaac blessing Jacob, c.1660
[Fig. 30]

Red and black chalk and brown wash, 14.9 x 21 cm.

Courtauld Gallery, London (Witt Collection)

An outstanding example of Jordaens's draughtsmanship, this is one of five drawings of *Isaac blessing Jacob* made by him around 1660. All appear to be compositional studies though, in the case of this work, no comparable painting is known. Jordaens's most celebrated canvas of this theme is in the Musée des Beaux-Arts, Lille, and dates from 1660.

In this drawing Isaac is depicted touching Jacob's head with his left hand and his hand with his right. This action

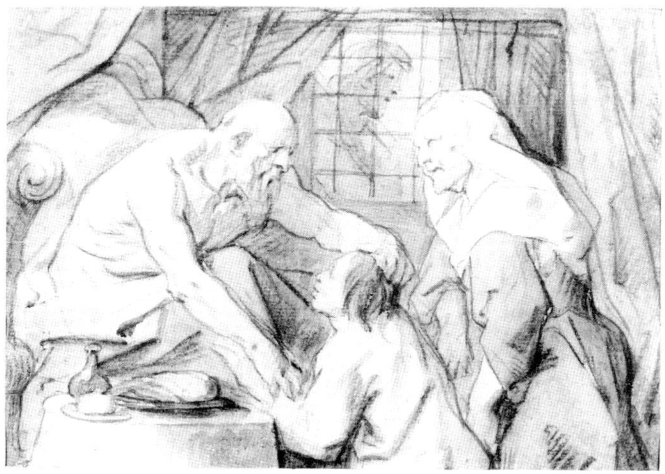

Fig. 30 (No. 20), Jacob Jordaens, *Isaac blessing Jacob*, Courtauld Gallery, London

occurs in the majority of Jordaens's works on this theme (including the canvas at Lille) and presumably represents the simultaneous act of establishing that Jacob is hairy and bestowing the blessing. Behind the kneeling youth Rebecca gazes watchfully on; while, through a window at the rear may be seen the figure of Esau, returning from the hunt.

The monumental treatment of the figure group, which is depicted three-quarter length and in the foreground plane, recalls that of both Dutch and Italian examples from earlier in the century, including that by Stom. Unique to Jordaens, however, is the muscular and heroic figure of Isaac, who is reminiscent of the biblical patriarchs of Rubens and may also owe something to a lost *Isaac blessing Jacob* by another Flemish master, Abraham Janssens, mentioned above (p. 26).

After Rubens and van Dyck, Jordaens was the greatest Flemish painter of the seventeenth century. He worked as Rubens's assistant in the late 1630s and perpetuated his florid and exuberant style long after the master's death in 1640.

Reference: R.–A. d'Hulst, *Jordaens Drawings*, London and New York, 1974, Vol. II, p. 445, no. A382.

21 Pieter de Jode the Younger (1601–after 1674), after Gerard Seghers

Christ and Nicodemus, c.1630
[Fig. 31]

Engraving, 28.4 x 32.3 cm.

The Barber Institute of Fine Arts, The University of Birmingham

This outstanding print is after a lost painting of c.1615 by Gerard Seghers (1591–1651), one of the leading Flemish painters of the first half of the seventeenth century. He became a master at the Antwerp Guild in 1608 and, early in the following decade, journeyed to Rome, where he was

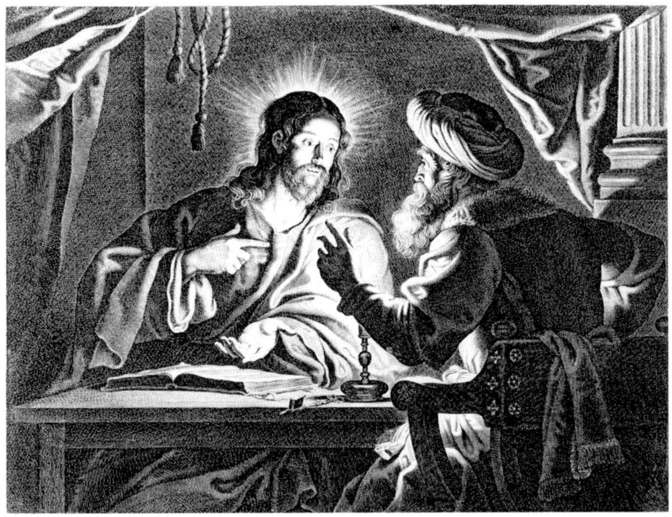

Fig. 31 (No. 21), Pieter de Jode the Younger (after Gerard Seghers), *Christ and Nicodemus*

deeply influenced by the art of Caravaggio and his Dutch followers – especially Honthorst and Baburen – who were then working in the city. After returning to Antwerp in (or before) 1620, he became increasingly attracted to the more colourful and extrovert style of Rubens.

Christ and Nicodemus is clearly a product of Seghers's Roman years and reveals his fascination with the dramatic lighting of Caravaggio's art and the candlelight effects favoured by many of his Dutch followers. The subject is from John III, 1–21. Nicodemus was a Pharisee and member of the council of Jews in Jerusalem. He is here shown visiting Christ by night and being instructed by him. The inscription at the bottom of the print records Christ's advice to him:

He asked him, to prove so great a teacher, "Is it possible for an old man to enter into his mother's womb?" Jesus replied, "Clearly, Nicodemus, a mystery lies hidden in these mystic forms of speech and worthy doctrines are concealed in any faith. Are you an ignorant slave? Yet the spirit will be able to be reborn from that very flesh. Believe this and you will be another Oedipus [solver of all riddles]."

Enlightened by Christ, Nicodemus subsequently assisted at his burial and is traditionally portrayed as a plainly dressed man, helping to lower Christ's body from the cross, accompanied by the more elegantly clad Joseph of Arimathea.

Stom also painted three versions of this subject (Nicolson, 1989, p. 182), doubtless attracted by the opportunity it afforded for portraying the dramatic effects of candlelight.

Reference: F.W. H. Hollstein, *Dutch and Flemish Etchings, Engravings and Woodcuts ca. 1450 – 1700*, Amsterdam, 1949, Vol. IX, p. 211, no. 12.

22 John Dean (c.1750–98), after William Dobson

Salome receiving the Head of John the Baptist, 1786
[Fig. 32]

Mezzotint, 53.2 x 43.4 cm.

Board of Trustees of the National Museums and Galleries on Merseyside (Walker Art Gallery, Liverpool)

This mezzotint is after Dobson's copy of Stom's *Salome receiving the Head of John the Baptist* (figs. 12 and 13) and was executed in 1786, when the former was in the Earl of Pembroke's collection. With the exception of the flame of

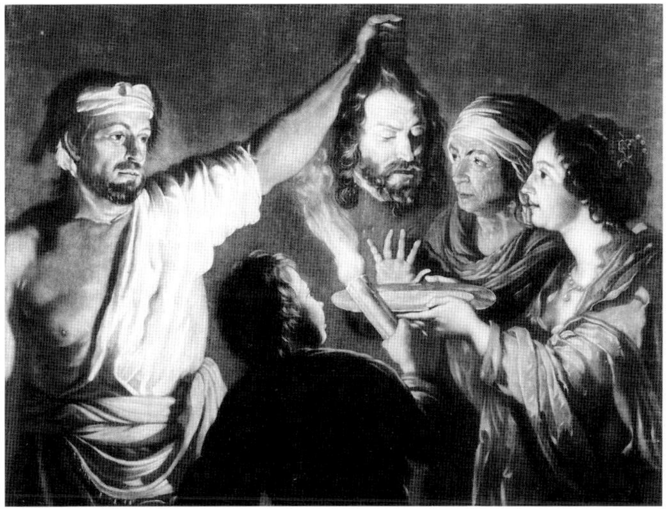

Fig. 32 (No. 22), John Dean (after William Dobson), *Salome receiving the Head of John the Baptist*

the torch held by the youth, which has been enlarged, it reproduces Dobson's painting accurately. The absence of the executioner's right arm from the print indicates that the original canvas had already been cut down by this date. The flickering play of light and shade of the original are ideally suited to mezzotint, a medium in which the entire plate is completely darkened and shapes and highlights are defined by scraping over this so that forms emerge from a black background.

23 Valentine Green (1739–1813), after Joseph Wright of Derby

Miravan breaking open the Tomb of his Ancestors, 1773
[Fig.33]

Mezzotint, 50.7 x 35.7 cm.

The Barber Institute of Fine Arts, The University of Birmingham

One of the greatest of all mezzotint engravers, Valentine Green specialised in making prints after Reynolds and the Old Masters, like his pupil John Dean (cf. fig. 32). This is one of only three mezzotints he executed after Joseph Wright of Derby (1734–97) and faithfully reproduces the latter's painting of the same title (Derby Museum and Art Gallery) of 1772.

The source of this gruesome moral tale has never been identified, but it may derive from a collection of Persian fairy tales. The young nobleman, Miravan, has been assured by an inscription on the tomb of his ancestors that, if he broke it open, he would find 'a greater treasure than even Croesus possessed'. Instead, when he did so, he discovered only a heap of bones and dust, together with an inscription berating him for his insatiable love of gold.

Inspired by the art of Honthorst and Terbrugghen, and by the later Dutch master of candlelight scenes Godfried Schalken (1643–1706), Wright portrays this scene taking place at night and lit only by the lurid rays of the moon and a single overhanging lamp. The Caravaggesque style enhances the mood of gothic horror of the tale and finds obvious parallels in the literature of this period. The vogue for such subjects also coincides closely in date with John Dean's mezzotint of another Caravaggesque work from the preceding century, Dobson's copy after Stom's *Salome receiving the Head of John the Baptist* (fig. 32).

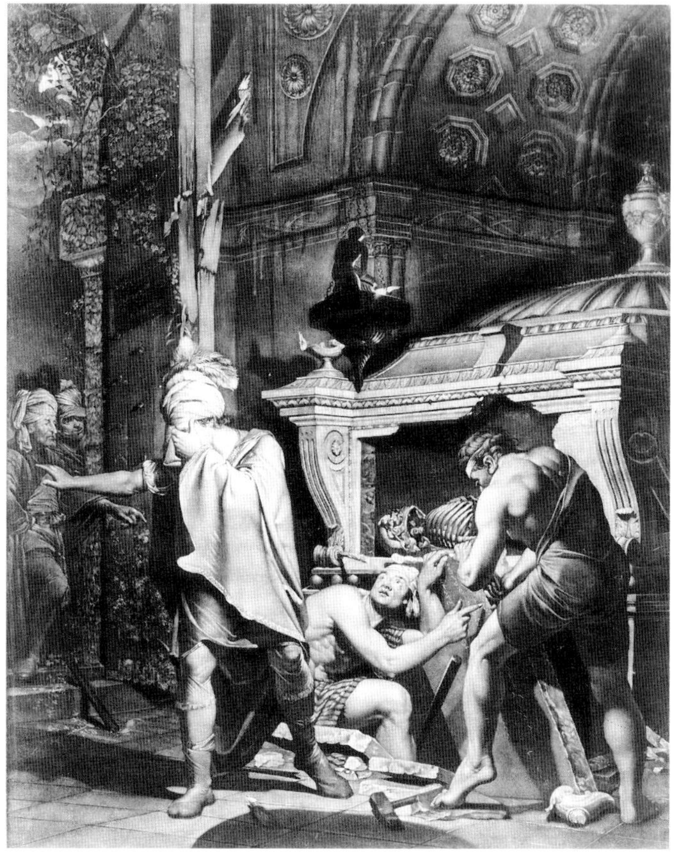

Fig. 33 (No. 23), Valentine Green
(after Joseph Wright of Derby),
Miravan breaking open the Tomb of his Ancestors

Nicolson's Stom brought up-to-date

Listed below are those paintings by (or attributed to) Stom that have come to light since the publication of Benedict Nicolson's *Caravaggism in Europe* in 1989 and any changes in location of works already listed by him. Works by followers are not included. This information has been compiled from the resources of the Witt Library, Courtauld Institute of Art, London, the Rijksbureau voor Kunsthistorische Documentatie (RKD), The Hague, and elsewhere. Given the frequency with which pictures by Stom change hands, however, it is unlikely to be complete. Entries follow the form established by Nicolson; dimensions are in centimetres, height before width.

Satyr and Peasant (two figures: not the Aesop subject)
With Athenaeum, Monte Carlo, 1987. Photo in Warburg Library (under Aesop, Satyr with Peasant Family).
Very early work.

Mucius Scaevola before Porsenna
Sale, Sotheby's, London, 13 July 1977 (190). 102 x 129.5.

Death of Seneca
Sale, Christie's, London, 30 November 1979 (12), illus.
63 x 86.5.

Adam and Eve
With Athenaeum, Monte Carlo; exh. Burlington Fine Art Fair, Royal Academy, London, 1979. Photo: RKD.

Sarah brings Hagar to Abraham
Sale, Sotheby's, London, 11 December 1991 (51), illus.
139 x 182.

Sacrifice of Isaac
Musée Fesch, Ajaccio Photo: RKD.

Isaac blessing Jacob
(Nicolson 1989, no. 1485)
The Barber Institute of Fine Arts, The University of Birmingham (1994.2).

Joseph interpreting Pharoah's dreams
Sale, Sotheby's, New York, 11 January 1990 (70), illus. 120.5 x 152.

Judgement of Solomon
Sale, Sotheby's, London, 11 December 1991 (68), illus. 157 x 222.

Tobias healing Tobit
(Nicolson 1989, no. 1561, 4)
Sale, Sotheby's, London, 9 December 1994 (372), illus. With Caretto, Turin, 1995.

Adoration of the Shepherds (six figures)
Formerly Earl of Malmesbury, Hurn Court, Christchurch, Hants; last traceable David Koetser, New York. Photo: RKD.

Adoration of the Shepherds (five figures)
Sale, Sotheby's, Monaco, 2–3 December 1989 (202), illus. 98 x 107.

Christ among the Doctors
(Nicolson 1989, p. 182, as Private Collection, Lugano)
Sale, Sotheby's, London, 5 July 1989 (7), illus. Collection of Mr. A. Alfred Taubman.

Christ and Nicodemus
(Nicolson 1989, p. 182, as formerly with Sestieri, Rome).
Sale, Sotheby's, New York, 15 January 1993 (225), illus. (as studio of Stomer).

The Tribute Money found in the fish
Sale, Phillips, London, 7 December 1993 (66), illus.
82.5 x 96.5. Variant of picture in the Palazzo Alliata Villafranca, Palermo (Nicolson 1989, p. 182). By follower?

Christ and the Adultress
Montreal Museum of Fine Arts (1993.16); exh. *Sinners and Saints, Darkness and Light, Caravaggio and his Dutch and Flemish Followers*, North Carolina Museum of Art, Raleigh, 1998, no. 37.

Christ's capture
Sale, Sotheby's, London, 16 April 1997 (152), illus. 71.9 x 84.

Christ before Caiaphas
(Nicolson 1989, no. 1464)
Sale, Stockholm Auktionsverk, 19 May 1998 (1454); Private Collection, Sweden.

Christ mocked
(Nicolson 1989, p. 183, as with Richard Feigen, New York)
Norton Simon Museum, Pasadena

Christ mocked
Sale, Sotheby's, London, 17 December 1994 (32), illus. 128 x 154. Follower?

Christ carrying the Cross
(Nicolson 1989, p. 183, as Private Collection, Budapest)
Sale, Sotheby's, London, 12 December 1990 (46), illus.; with Colnaghi; sale, Wiener Kunst Auktionen, 10 January 1996 (17).

St Cecilia and the Angel
(Nicolson 1989, no. 1501)
Sale, Christie's, London, 29 June 1979 (81), illus.

St Gregory the Great
(Nicolson 1989, p. 184, as Private Collection, Paris)
With Galerie de la Scala, Paris, 1992.

St Jerome
Exh. Harari and Johns, London, November – December 1989, no. 38. 87.9 x 117.3.

St Jerome listening to Trumpet
Sale, Sotheby's, London, 3 June 1981 (63), illus., as attr. H. van Somer but by Stom. 130.5 x 79.

St Jerome listening to Trumpet
Sale, Sotheby's, New York, 30 May 1991 (44), illus.; Christie's, New York, 14 January 1993 (174), illus.; Private Collection, Philadelphia. 93.3 x 122.6.

St Matthew's Calling
(Nicolson 1989, no. 1557)
The Fine Arts Museums of San Francisco (1986.27); exh. *Sinners and Saints, Darkness and Light, Caravaggio and his Dutch and Flemish Followers*, North Carolina Museum of Art, Raleigh, 1998, no. 36.

St Onuphrius
(Nicolson 1989, no. 1496)
Sale, Christie's London, 11 December 1992 (12) and 10 July 1998 (239), illus.

St Peter repentant by candlelight
(Nicolson 1989, p. 186, as sale, Sotheby's, Monaco, 1984) With K. and V. Waterman, Amsterdam, 1994; exh. *Holländische Malerei in neuem Licht, Hendrick ter Brugghen und seine Zeitgenossen*, Centraal Museum, Utrecht, and Herzog Anton Ulrich-Museum, Braunschweig, 1986–7, no. 78.

St Peter in Jail
Sale, Sotheby's, London, 31 October 1990 (180), illus. 89.5 x 126.

Saints Peter and Cleophas
Sale, Sotheby's, London, 12 December 1990 (211), illus. 96.5 x 66. Fragment of a *Supper at Emmaus*.

Man with Flute
(Nicolson 1989, p. 186, as with Duits, London, 1927)
Collection Mr. and Mrs. John L. Stainton; exh. *Sinners and Saints, Darkness and Light, Caravaggio and his Dutch and Flemish Followers*, North Carolina Museum of Art, Raleigh, 1998, no. 39.

Boy reading by candlelight
(Nicolson 1989, p. 186, no. 1480)
Nationalmuseum, Stockholm; exh. *Rembrandt och hans tid (Rembrandt and his age)*, Nationalmuseum, Stockholm, 1992–3, no. 12.

Old Woman and Man (she with beads, he with hot coals).
Sale, Christie's London, 13 December 1991 (37), illus.
94 x 116.5.

Old Woman with coins by lamplight
Sale, Sotheby's, New York, 11 January 1996 (77), illus.
67.9 x 57.5.

Old Woman with chalice and stick
(Nicolson 1989, no. 1521)
Sale, Sotheby's, Monaco, 2–3 December 1989 (304), illus.

Soldier lighting pipe from oil lamp
(Nicolson 1989, p. 187, as Principe di Galati Collection, Palermo)
Sale, Sotheby's, New York, 17 January 1992 (46A), illus., as pendant to a *Young Woman holding a distaff* by Adam de Coster.

Selected Bibliography

Caravaggio in Sicilia: Il suo tempo, il suo influsso, Palazzo Bellomo, Syracuse, 1984, pp. 208–11, 235–47.

Holländische Malerei in neuem Licht, Hendrick ter Brugghen und seine Zeitgenossen, Centraal Museum, Utrecht, and Herzog Anton Ulrich-Museum, Braunschweig, 1986–87, pp. 333–44, nos. 75–8.

Nicolson, Benedict, 'Stomer brought up-to-date', *The Burlington Magazine* CXIX, April 1977, pp. 230–45.

Nicolson, Benedict, *The International Caravaggesque Movement*, Oxford, 1979.

Nicolson, Benedict, *Caravaggism in Europe*, second edition, revised and enlarged by Luisa Vertova, Turin, 1989. 3 vols.

Pauwels, H., 'De Schilder Matthias Stomer', *Gentse Bijdragen tot de Kunstgeschiedenis*, XIV, 1953, pp. 139–92.

Pauwels, H., 'Nieuwe Toeschrijvingen aan M. Stomer', *Gentse Bijdragen tot de Kunstgeschiedenis*, XV, 1954, pp. 233–40.

Schneider, A. von, *Caravaggio und die Niederländer*, 2nd edition, Amsterdam, 1967, pp. 116–23.

Sinners and Saints, Darkness and Light, Caravaggio and his Dutch and Flemish Followers, by Dennis P. Weller, North Carolina Museum of Art, Raleigh, 1998, pp. 191–204, nos. 36–9 and *passim*.

Slatkes, Leonard J., 'Matthias Stom', *The Dictionary of Art*, London, 1996, Vol. 29, pp. 696–8.

Spear, Richard E., *Caravaggio and his Followers*, revised edition, New York, 1975, pp. 168–71.

Voss, Hermann, 'Charakterköpfe des Seicento II: Matthäus Stomer', *Monatshefte für Kunstwissenschaft*, 1908, pp. 990–99.

Voss, Hermann, 'Charakterköpfe des Seicento III: Der Meister des Sterbenden Cato', *Monatshefte für Kunstwissenschaft*, 1909, pp. 108–15.

Walsh Jr., John, 'Stomer's Evangelists', *The Burlington Magazine*, CXVIII, July 1976, pp. 504, 507–8.

Photographic Credits

Fig. 2 Mr. A. Alfred Taubman

Fig. 5 Courtesy of the National Gallery of Ireland

Fig. 10 Rijksmuseum-Stichting, Amsterdam

Fig. 16 © Photo Réunion des musées nationaux, Paris

Fig. 21 © National Gallery, London

Fig. 28 Devonshire Collection, Chatsworth. Reproduced by permission of the Duke of Devonshire and the Chatsworth Settlement Trustees. Photograph: Photographic Survey, Courtauld Institute of Art